IMMIGRATION:
Here They Are Ready or Not

NORMAN F. BOURKE
MEMORIAL LIBRARY
CAYUGA
COMMUNITY COLLEGE
AUBURN, NEW YORK 13021

Barbed Wire Image: This file is licensed under the
Creative Commons Attribution-Share Alike 3.0 Unported license.

Copyright © 2011 Bob Ritz
All rights reserved.

ISBN-10: 1450553672
EAN-13: 9781450553674

IMMIGRATION: Here They Are Ready or Not

Bob Ritz

There's a place where I've been told,
Every street is paved with gold,
And it's just across the borderline.

Ry Cooder[1]

for
Blaine,
Ralph, Alex, and Courtney,
and Frank, Clark, and Kevin, who know how to do their sums.

Contents

**Preface, A SYNTHESIS OF THINGS NOT
   COMMONLY PUT TOGETHER** xi

Acknowledgments xv

Introduction xvii

Chapter One, MIGRATION BASICS 1

Chapter Two, QUOTAS AND VISAS 11
   Give Me Your Tired 11
   Quotas and Visas 12
   Immigrant Visas 13
   Non-Immigrant Visas 15
   Refugees and Asylees 17

Chapter Three, CITIZENSHIP 21
   Virtual Citizens 21
   "Anchor Babies" 23
   Undocumented Children 23
   The Dream Act 24
   Routes to U.S. Citizenship 25

Chapter Four, POPULATION AND SOCIAL SECURITY 31
   Migrants 31
   Boomers 33
   Social Security and the Graying of America 36

Chapter Five, CRIME 45
   Statistical Problems with Reporting Hispanic Crime 45
   Hispanic Crime - General 47
   Incarceration of Hispanics 48
   Capital Crimes by Hispanics 49

    Legal Responses... 50
    Pseudo Crime.. 52
    Removal 53

Chapter Six, NATIONAL SECURITY 59
    The U.S. Immigration and Customs Enforcement Service (ICE) .. 59
    Border Security 60
    Drugs 61
    Terrorists... 62
    The Virtual Wall... 64
    Documentation for Migrants 67
    E-Verify for Employers....................................... 68
    Real ID for United States Citizens 69

Chapter Seven, ASSIMILATION 75
    Assimilation 75
    Barrios and Borderlands...................................... 76
    "No Interest" Mexican Credit................................. 78
    Driving While Brown.. 78
    Politics, Business, and Religion............................. 80
    Migrants and Welfare 82

Chapter Eight, THE ECONOMY 87
    Coyotes 87
    Dying to Work 89
    "They're Here to Take Our Jobs".............................. 91
    Cash or Credit?.. 95
    Remittances 97

Chapter Nine, NAFTA 103
    Trading Blocs 103
    Maquiladoras 105
    Organized Labor 108
    Free-Range Trucking... 109

Chapter Ten, GUEST WORKER PROGRAMS 115

CONCLUSIONS 125

Appendices **131**
    A - The Statue of Liberty 133
    B - The Mexican-American Boundary Survey 137
    C - Non-Citizens and Voting 141
    D - Bilingual Education 145
    E - English as the National Language. 149
    F - Sample U.S. Citizenship Exam with Answers 153
    G - Famous Immigrants. 155
    H - Not All American Heroes Have Been American 159
    I - And the Boy Became A Man. 163

Bibliography **167**

Preface

A Synthesis of Things Not Commonly Put Together

POLITICAL CORRECTNESS SACRIFICES accuracy and distorts history, so I have tried not to be politically correct. People on the left delight in saying that Mexicans take jobs that Americans don't want. That may be politically correct, but it is not true. Mexicans take jobs that Americans don't want their neighbors to *see* them doing, even though some of those jobs pay quite well.

The language of this book reflects the primary realities of immigration to the United States – young, male, and Mexican (Mexicans are sixty-two percent of those entering since 2000).[2] We are told this cohort steals jobs, drives crime, and abuses welfare and health care. I have not intentionally written from the left or from the right, but as a middle-of-the-road-radical. There is something here for everyone to love or hate.

My interest in immigration began while taking simultaneous degrees in horticulture and Spanish. This led to an article in *American Nurseryman* magazine where I promoted the idea of Spanish as an elective for horticulture and agriculture students. My research only identified a few schools that would even consider Spanish as an elective. That is not the case now. Later I studied at the *Instituto Technologico Agropecuario* in Conkal, Yucatan, Mexico – class in the morning followed by fieldwork in the afternoon. My bachelor's and master's degrees attempted to duplicate programs at universities that offered borderlands or immigration studies. My master's degree also included some crossover study in the college of law.

Academia and work in extension programs in two different countries provided different perspectives. Another invaluable experience was living in a community of undocumented workers. This does not mean that I always shared their opinions, but I do appreciate their issues.

Immigration is much like the study of fractals. Both are infinite, and neither can be understood at a glance. Also, statistically reliable conclusions cannot be reached in the absence of statistically reliable data, so I found many immigration statistics too disparate to be of much use. The best anyone seems to be able to say about statistics is that they "suggest" this or that, even if no one is quite sure what they suggest.[3] That is reason enough to ignore most of them.

From pre-publication to post-publication, laws will change and research will be contradicted by other research or challenged on methodological grounds. Government statistics are often politically motivated. The federal government can't accurately estimate the number of undocumented residents, immigration lawyers have difficulty keeping up with rapidly changing immigration laws, and "think tank" scholars can't agree on the meaning of it all. Further, many studies take years to produce and may appear dated when they are actually the most recent information available. Finally, poll-driven politicians continue in the time-honored tradition of holding a moistened finger to the wind.

My original idea was to compile class notes from my years as a student with notes from the various classes which I now teach, especially Latin American History and Immigration Law. What emerged instead was a historical, legal, cultural, and practical overview on immigration for the average reader. Unlike a book that begins and ends in some logical fashion, the immigration debate is still unfolding, it is not linear, and it seldom appears to be logical. *Here They Are, Ready or Not* does not have to be read from front to back. The subject matter is too diverse to require that kind of organization. Rather, like a paint-by-numbers set, a clear picture should emerge however it is read.

Readers who need more information on immigration can access the websites of various public and private organizations. (When trying to contact a government agency, do not use the 1-800-FED-INFO listing in your telephone directory. Their only purpose is to run interference for government agencies so their employees can work without being bothered by you. FED-INFO operators will even refuse to give you mailing addresses for government agencies. Calling the office of your U.S. Congressmen or Senator will yield much better results, much faster.)

This book is not meant to be anyone's final word. Most of us will never have the same understanding of immigration as a migrant, a border patrol officer, a *coyote*, residents on either side of the border, or any of the other players. What I offer is a synthesis of things not commonly put together. I hope it is more informative than what you get from demagogues who are paid by the decibel.

Finally, Abraham Lincoln's words are perfectly applicable to the current immigration debate, "The struggle of today is not altogether for today. It is for a vast future, also."[1]

Bob Ritz
January 2012

Acknowledgements

FOR SEVERAL YEARS early in my study of immigration I had no real understanding of what I was about. I was sure that it was important, but I could not say why. Worse yet, no one else thought it was important.

No one can write a book without help from many people. In my case this included someone I never met. During my unfocused period, my car radio, which had not worked in years, suddenly came on, tuned to National Public Radio. Ray Suarez was hosting a program about migrant farm workers. At that moment, everything came into focus – not so much about migrant farm workers, *per se*, but about immigration studies in general.

My thanks also go to four extraordinary college professors who gave me encouragement after I realized that immigration was a legitimate field of inquiry. From Jim Bohlmann at Tulsa Community College, I learned more than crop sciences. He was the first, and for many years the only professor who recognized that my interest in immigration was academically sound. Thanks to Lillian McConnell at Langston University, I was able to begin a synthesized specialization in immigration studies as an undergraduate student. She also taught me not to say "a lot." At the graduate level at the University of Tulsa, I received encouragement from Dr. Thomas Buckley, and in the University's College of Law, I profited from Cynthia Hess who helped me to understand the complexities of immigration law and procedure. Her death in 2009 has deprived future generations of students of her expertise and her humor.

Raymond DeBrosse and Sergio Garcia gave my manuscript a first reading. Brian McFarland cleaned up some sloppy government statistics. Gary Goode performed two edits. Daniel Chaboya was helpful throughout. Alfredo Montelongo was an invaluable resource and an exemplar of the U.S. Border Patrol. My brother, Dr. Ralph Ritz, had faith in me when I enrolled in graduate school, offered encouragement when I decided to teach, and believed in me when I said I was going to write this book. Vincent Blaine's whimsical photographic art appears throughout this book. I am partial to his work. Any father would be.

Introduction

IN LATE SPRING 2007, the United States faced an increasingly unpopular war in Iraq, concerns over the nuclear intentions of Iran and North Korea, and the never-ending unrest between Israel and Palestine. At home, President Bush and his Republican allies in Congress had failed in their quest for a domestic legacy, and the Democrats had failed to stop the war in Iraq.

Suddenly, illegal migration emerged as a pressing domestic issue. Marshalltown, Iowa and Hazelton, Pennsylvania represented a modern day *Tale of Two Cities*. Beginning in 2000, Iowa, whose population had been declining for more than twenty years, began soliciting immigrants by billing itself as "The Ellis Island of the Midwest." Hazelton, Pennsylvania on the other hand, was the first American city to attempt municipal control of immigration by claiming an unproven Hispanic crime wave. Many states and municipalities followed Hazelton's lead. Their ordinances were usually based on fear of crime and lowered property values, even if these fears were unsubstantiated.

No one copied Iowa's example until 2011 when Dayton Ohio began a similar campaign. Now, other cities are considering immigration as a partial solution to population decline.

The United States had not passed any new immigration legislation since 1996. Few people, inside or outside of government, had any idea of what was about to take place. No journalist, academic, or talk show host expected any movement on immigration reform until at least 2009.

What happened was a unique moment in U.S. history. George Bush, a lame duck president, Ted Kennedy, his political nemesis, and a bipartisan group of senators, introduced an immigration bill in the U.S. Senate that both parties thought would position them for victory in the elections of 2008.

The Senate group claimed to have worked in secret in order to avoid the influence of lobbyists and special interest groups. In reality, it was the American public that was avoided, while the lobbyists and special interest groups had their way as usual.

The resulting bill was a 380-page mishmash of unpopular, unworkable legislation, promoted by the special interest groups. For example, migrants wanting to legalize their status would have to return to their homeland and pay back U.S. taxes plus fines in excess of $8,000, in addition to paying $1,010 for a "green card" (triple the fee for 2006). In Mexico, where the average wage is about two dollars a day, only a drug dealer could come up with that amount of money. The provision for people to leave and re-enter the country was actually a ruse to get them out and keep them out.

The bill was withdrawn from consideration after it became clear that a majority in neither party would support it. A few weeks later, a superficially reworked version was introduced, but it also failed to garner the necessary support required for passage.

The main components of both bills were securing the nation's southern border, sanctions against employers who hired illegal workers, and an unpopular amnesty for twelve million or more people residing illegally in the United States. The Department of Homeland Security, which reports directly to the White House, began a series of highly publicized immigration raids on bus stations, packinghouses, and other locations where large numbers of undocumented migrants were likely to be found.

However, in trying to remove undocumented migrants from the country, the Department of Homeland Security works against the interests of the Social Security Administration, which counts on payroll deductions from workers who will never be able to claim any benefits from their contributions. Based on years of experience, the Social Security Administration includes these amounts in its annual projections.

The public's lack of information on immigration was, and continues to be appalling. Talk show hosts could have addressed real immigration concerns, such as the 5,525-mile border between the United States and Canada, or 12,479 miles of easily penetrable U.S. coastline, but they made no effort to do so.[5] Instead, they poisoned public opinion against real reform which Americans said they wanted. Even so, immigrant bashing had the opposite of the intended effect on the 2006 mid-term elections, with rabid immigration haters losing elections all over the country. More recently, a recall petition in 2011 removed the caustic and divisive Arizona Senate president Russell Pearce from office. Pearce was the principal author of that state's anti-immigrant legislation.

Both candidates in the 2008 presidential race promised they would do something about immigration reform if elected. The worldwide financial crisis and the debate over health care reform has forestalled any meaningful action by the Obama presidency.

Notes

[1] Ry Cooder, "Across the Borderline," Lyrics by Ry Cooder (Universal Music Publishing Group, 1995).

[2] United States. Office of Homeland Security, Estimates of the Unauthorized Immigrant Population Residing in the United States: January 2010. (Washington, GPO: 2011)1, 4. The primary sending countries, in descending order are Mexico, El Salvador, Guatemala, Honduras, Philippines, India, Ecuador, Brazil, South Korea, and China. The primary receiving states, in descending order are California, Texas, Florida, Illinois, Arizona, Georgia, New York, North Carolina, New Jersey, and Nevada.

[3] Suggested by Earl Shorris, Latinos (New York: W. W. Norton, 1972), 179.

[4] Abraham Lincoln, "Annual Message to Congress, 3 December 1861," Collected Works of Abraham Lincoln. Volume 5, 1861-1862, Ed. Roy P. Basler (Piscataway, NJ: Rutgers UP), 35-54.

[5] United States. CRS Report to Congress, United States International Borders: Briefacts, by Janice Cheryl Beaver (Washington: GPO, 2006).

Chapter One

Migration Basics

> *They come without proper papers. Most of them have no intention of assimilating into our culture. Language, religion, tradition, history, manners, politics, appearance and expectations separate us. The illegals obey the law only when it is convenient for them.*
> Manuel G. Gonzalez[1]

LIKE THE POOR, migrants have always been with us. However, in the example above, the illegal sojourners were not Mexicans sneaking into the United States, but Americans sneaking into Texas when it was still a part of Mexico. One of these interlopers was Joseph Louis Fox, from Cincinnati, Ohio. Fox was the Irish-American grandfather of Mexican President Vicente Fox.[2]

* * *

Migrants come to America from all parts of the world, but historically, first world countries get natural resources from the third world, and labor from the second. Mexico and Central America have always been the primary pools for labor imported into the United States, and the American economy will require their services for at least another forty years.

Most attention is focused on Mexican migrants, especially those who are here illegally. The current wave of Mexican migration followed an earthquake in Mexico City in 1985, Ronald Reagan's amnesty for 2.7 million seasonal agricultural workers in 1986, the devaluation of the Mexican peso, and a scandal in the Mexican presidential elections, both in 1994.

What should the United States do in the future to deal with migration? One option would be to start by viewing it as an opportunity instead of a problem, one that has often been badly managed, but one that has always sorted itself out.

Conflicting perspectives will always be held by different members in a community. To be competitive, a commercial grower may hire undocumented workers. A teacher might be concerned about the increasing enrollment of Spanish-speaking children in her classroom, but she enjoys fresh produce. Migrant workers are concerned for the welfare of their families. The border patrol must enforce the law. Politicians must stand for reelection.

All but this last perspective must be seriously considered for the immigration debate to move forward, but too often the priorities are reversed.

Why do people forsake their native land, their homes, their families, friends, and familiar surroundings, even risking death for an uncertain future north of the border? Sometimes migrants come to the United States for temporary arrangements that only involve their labor. In this case, the migrant's only goal is to make money. Others migrate because they want to better themselves on a more permanent basis. Money is a certainly factor, but more opportunities, a better quality of life, education for their children, and a longer life expectancy are also considerations.

Man has migrated since the beginning of history. Migration is common to all societies, even if it is only internal migration. The founding fathers emigrated from the British Isles and Europe. Irish citizens emigrated following the potato famine of 1840.[3] Chinese and Mexican migrants followed. Southern European immigration persisted until the 1920s. Since World War II, the United States has experienced migrations from Southeast Asia, Cuba, South Korea, and India. Each group has faced discrimination to a greater or lesser degree, usually from the group that immediately preceded it.

Mexicans and Other-Than-Mexicans (OTMs) from Central America comprise seventy-eight percent of the existing migrant population in the United States. In the last quarter of a century, Mexicans have migrated in large numbers and they represent most of the migrant flow.[4] OTMs from Central America provide infill into the south of Mexico that partially offsets Mexican outflow in the north.

Immigration law has developed with the passage of time. Until the late 1800s, it was considered a matter for the states.[5] The U.S. Constitution does not expressly authorize the federal government to regulate immigration, but it has come to be understood as one of the plenary powers of Congress, and is it has generally been exempt from constitutional scrutiny. Immigration also operates under the concept of "field preemption," meaning that federal laws trump state or local laws.[6]

A **migrant** is a person who travels from his place of habitual residence, crossing one or more major jurisdictional boundaries (such as a state, national, or international border), and who resides in a new place for at least one year.[7] Migrants tend to seek new locations similar to their previous home, where their journey is not impeded by oceans, large rivers, deserts, or mountain ranges.

The common usage of the term is when it is applied to "migrant workers," usually agricultural workers, who travel from one location to another following planting and harvest schedules. However, this usage ignores the requirement of remaining in one place for a year unless these workers are migrants in the sense that they remain in the United States for one year. Any worker who comes here (legally or illegally) and remains for one year must, by definition, be a migrant.

In dealing with people of unknown status, no word is perfect, but "migrant" covers most situations best. When a specific status is known, or when there is some reason critical to discussion, the terms emigrant, immigrant, non-citizen, undocumented/*indocumentado,* or guest worker may be used. "Migrant" will be used in this book as a blanket description even though the usage is unfamiliar to the American ear.

An *e***migrant** is a migrant measured from the perspective of the parent, or sending country. An *im***migrant** is measured from the perspective of the host, or receiving country.

Immigrants are migrants who come here legally and who intend to remain in the United States, with or without pursuing citizenship, making **illegal immigrant** an oxymoron. Since the movie "*E. T.,*" **illegal alien** has fallen from government favor, although not from popular usage.

Also, referring to undocumented children as being "illegal" is incorrect for the same reason that referring to a baby born out of wedlock as "illegitimate" is incorrect (see Chapter Three). The baby did not do anything illegal. Similarly, no person is "illegal;" criminal acts are illegal, but people are not.

Wetback (*mojado*) and other pejoratives are still in use in some quarters.

A **commuter** is a migrant, legal or otherwise, who travels back and forth across the border on a daily basis for the sake of employment. The legal commuters use so-called "laser visas" to go back and forth. As long as they do not cross a border to be strikebreakers, no one pays much attention to them.[8] Day laborers are sometimes called *jornaleros*.

Non-citizens may be here legally, such as a student or a tourist, or their presence may be other than legal. The bureaucratic term for a non-citizens who are not here legally is **EWI** ("Entered without Inspection"), although they are generally referred to as being **undocumented/*indocumentado***. The term undocumented does not mean that they have no documents; they just do not have the documents that the United States requires for a person to be here legally, such as a passport, a visa, an employment authorization, or a permanent resident card ("green card").

Undocumented workers may have a birth certificate, a Baptismal certificate, a foreign driver's license, or, if they are from Mexico, a "*Matricula Consular*" (see Chapter Six). However, migrants crossing the border illegally do not carry their documents with them for two reasons. First is the fear of having them stolen by criminals or corrupt government authorities. Border crossers wait until they are safely at their destination, then have their documents mailed to them. The second reason is that if migrants do not have papers identifying them as being from a particular place, the border patrol will release them at the Mexican border, not knowing where else to send them. The migrants will not have to return to their homes in southern Mexico or Central America to begin their long journey all over again.

A **first-generation migrant** is a person who was not born in this country, although some of them have been here for so long that it doesn't make much sense to continue calling them "migrants." Their offspring, who *were* born in the United States, are referred to as the **second-generation**, and they are U.S. citizens by virtue of the Fourteenth Amendment to the Constitution.

* * *

Photo Credit: Vincent Blaine

The two main theories of immigration are the **push** and **pull** theories. A push could result from political unrest, years of successive crop failures, high unemployment, war, or some other negative situation. Some of the migration that the United States is currently experiencing from Latin America might be a delayed push away from the corrupt, right-wing Latin American dictatorships that the United States has supported since the 1950s.

A pull is usually employment, family ties or the chance for a better life. Push and pull work together, but pull dominates. While a person may desperately want to escape from his present situation (push), some reasonably certain alternative must await at the intended destination (pull). A migrant would not migrate to a country that was in the throes of a depression, or where he was likely to be imprisoned or killed.

For many migrants, low-wage work in the United States is a better option than remaining in their native country, being forced to join the armed forces or a guerrilla movement, working in a sweatshop, or street life: selling drugs, begging, stealing, or prostitution.

Migrants are self-chosen. For this reason, slaves and their descendants are not immigrants. **Exiles** (such as the "Cuban exiles") are also not immigrants if they profess a continuing loyalty to their homeland, and would prefer to return there after some undesirable circumstance is remedied.

Historically, migrants have been slightly better educated than the countrymen they leave behind.[9] Because people are not normally anxious to leave places that are familiar, migrants are more motivated and more optimistic than non-migrants. Once in a new country, these qualities express themselves in a greater entrepreneurial spirit than evident in the host population.

Worldwide migration, legal or otherwise, may be as high as 200 million people annually. The number of foreign-born residents in the United States, legal and illegal, may be as high as forty-three million.[10] Estimates suggest that Mexicans account for fifty-six percent of this population, or twenty four million people.[11] Other estimates are higher.

Estimates of undocumented persons living in the United States run between eight to twenty million, virtually all are Mexican or Central American. Approximately twelve million was the generally agreed upon number for several years.[12] However, many migrants appear to have returned home after the worldwide financial crisis of the past decade, dropping the estimates to 10.8 million.[13]

Estimates of the number of undocumented people who have entered the country in recent years go as high as a quarter to a half million migrants per year. Most of these people crossed the border illegally, although some came legally and overstayed their visas. The U.S. Border Patrol estimates that 115,000 unaccompanied children, some as young as six or seven, from El Salvador, Guatemala, Honduras, and Mexico cross the border each year.[14] In 2005, 6,460 underage foreign children were detained in U.S. government shelters. *Enrique's Journey*, the story of a Honduran child who got through, won two Pulitzer Prizes for its author, Sonia Nazario. Because of those like Enrique who get through, Mexico patrols its southern border with Guatemala diligently, unlike its attitude toward its northern border with the United States. Mexico sent 3,772 Guatemalan children back to Guatemala during 2005.[15]

* * *

The United States is the fifth largest Spanish-speaking country in the world, and Hispanics have now eclipsed blacks as the dominant minority.[16] The word **Hispanic** is a language-based term. There is some debate over whether it should be used as a noun or an adjective. In this book, it is used both ways. **Hispanic** includes everyone living in the United States whose native language is Spanish. By definition, there are no Hispanics in Latin America; Hispanics can only exist in the United States. Migrants from Brazil, Guyana, and Belize are not Hispanic because their native language is not Spanish.

Additionally, the term does not denote race. Hispanics can be any race, although they become members of a socially imposed race when Caucasian Americans want them to be. Mexicans, the largest migrant group in the U.S., are predominately *Mestizos*, that is, part Spaniard, and part Indian.

Except, for some unknown reason in 1930 census, the United States has classified persons of Mexican birth or ancestry who are not definitely Indian or some other non-white stock as Caucasian. Since 2000, the U.S. Census Bureau has allowed respondents to list more than one race on their census questionnaires. A Spanish-speaking Guatemalan of Mayan descent living in the United States could be classified as Indian-Hispanic. In Cuba, roughly half the population is black, so in the United States, those Cubans would be considered black-Hispanic. (The Cubans who left their island when Fidel Castro came to power were overwhelmingly Caucasian and many stateside *Cubanos* still discriminate against their black brethren.) Alberto Fujimora, a former president of Peru has Asian lineage.

The term Hispanic also suggests a monolithic culture, but this is not true. Puerto Ricans (who are U.S. citizens) and Dominicans (who are not) reside primarily on the east coast. Most Puerto Ricans are registered as Democratic voters. Cubans have congregated in Miami, Florida, ninety miles from their homeland. Most Cubans are registered as Republicans. Mexican Americans and Central Americans populate western states along the Mexican-American border. Their voting habits are unpredictable. These groups are historically and culturally diverse—their diets are different and they do not celebrate the same holidays. The Spanish language is the only thing these groups have in common.

The proper way to address members of this group is somewhat arbitrary. The term **Latino(a)** is still in use. **Chicano(a)** has had a checkered career, but is not as popular now as it once was. **Mexican-American** is the overwhelming favorite for that group, but compound names for other migrants are unwieldy (El Salvadoran-American, etc). Americans have felt an obligation to honor self-chosen names for various groups, such as Native Americans, blacks/African Americans, and gays. It is ironic that **Hispanic**, an artificial term, has more currency than any of the traditional or self-chosen terms.[17]

Notes

1 Suggested by Manuel G. Gonzales, Mexicanos: A History of Mexicans in the United States (Bloomington: Indiana UP, 1999), 70.

2 Alma Guillermoprieto, Looking for History: Dispatches from Latin America (New York: Pantheon-Random House, 2001), 287.

3 Ireland, historically a country of out-migration, is becoming a land of in-migration. Immigration, primarily from Poles, Romanians, and Bosnians, is not without unique and significant challenges for the Emerald Isle.

4 Jeffrey S. Passel, Size and Characteristics of the Unauthorized Migrant Population in the U.S. (based on March 2005 Population Survey), 15 Jan 2008, 20 Jan 2008 <http://pewhispanic.org/files/reports/61pdf>.

5 Stephen H. Legomsky, Overview, Immigration and Refugee Law and Policy, 3rd ed. (New York: Foundation Press, 2002), 2.

6 Legomsky, Immigration, 10, 152.

7 John R. Weeks, Population (Belmont: Wadsworth, 1999), 234.

8 Ruben Martinez, Crossing Over: A Mexican Family on the Migrant Trail (New York: St. Martins-Holtzbrinck, 2001), 179.

9 Weeks, Population, 242.

10 United States. U.S. Census Bureau, Current Population Survey (Washington: GPO, 2006).

11 Ruben G. Rumbaut, and Walter Ewing. Special Report: The Myth of Immigrant Criminality and the Paradox of Assimilation: Incarceration Rates among Native and Foreign-Born Men (Immigration Policy Center, A Division of the American Immigration Law Foundation, Spring 2007), 4.

12 Rumbaut, Special Report, 4.

13 United States. Office of Homeland Security, Estimates of the Unauthorized Immigrant Population Residing in the United States. (Washington, GPO: 2010) 2.

14 Peter Prengaman, "Immigrant Minors in Legal Limbo," Wall Street Journal (AP), 16-17 Sep 2006: 4.

15 N. C. Aizenman, "Young Migrants Risk All to Reach U.S.: Thousands Detained After Setting Out from Central America without Parents," Washington Post 28 Feb 2006, 27 Aug 2006 <http://www.washingtonpost.com/wp-dyn/content/article>.

16 Marty Knorre, Thallia Dorwick, William R. Glass, and Hildebrand Villarreal, Puntos de Partida, 4th ed. (New York: McGraw-Hill, 1993), 17.

17 The probable etiology of the word "Hispanic" is that it was conceived by a U.S. Commerce Department employee in anticipation of the 1970 Census. It is believed that Richard Nixon wanted a way to statistically group together Mexican Americans, Puerto Ricans, Dominicans, and Cubans for political purposes.

Chapter Two

Photo Credit: Vincent Blaine

Quotas and Visas

"Give Me Your Tired"

From the Civil War to the 1920s, immigrants, especially European immigrants, were welcomed with ease of admission and easy acquisition of rights.[1] Congress enacted rules of citizenship that made it easy for large numbers of European immigrants to gain entrance, citizenship, and suffrage well into the nineteenth century.[2] Immigrants did not need papers, just someone to vouch for them when they arrived, if that. Once simple, immigration law is now as complicated as the tax code, perhaps more so because it involves people.

The familiar words on the Statue of Liberty unofficially represented U.S. immigration policy for many decades (see Appendix A). Today, Americans would prefer that "the tired, the poor, the huddled masses, and the wretched refuse" were not quite so tired, so poor, or so wretched. Many Americans prefer that offers for the tired and the poor be for a limited time only, with more severe terms applied to the wretched.[3] In 125 years, the United States has gone from soliciting the tired, et al, to showing a distinct preference for nuclear physicists, computer programmers, physicians, mathematicians, and other highly trained professionals.

Migrants come here to work. Despite what the song says, love does not make the world go around, money does—dollars, yuans, pounds, rupees, yen, pesos, and euros. Most migrants think that dollars make the world go around the best, which is why they migrate to the U.S. instead of other to places.

Quotas and Visas

The International Declaration of Human Rights recognizes the right of people to migrate. Legal exercise of this right is not only contingent on the laws of the sending and receiving countries, but also on the laws of any country necessary for through passage.

In the United States, the number of immigrants who are admissible from a given country changes annually. The present quota system, enacted in 1965, prescribes a complicated system for immigration based on how many people from a given country are already here. Arguably, the quota system is the major cause of illegal migration: Mexico, Cuba, India, South Korea, and the Philippines have mortgaged their quotas far into the future. The current backlog is over four million applicants, and the wait can take a decade or longer.

Admission to the United States is a privilege, not a right.[4] The only people who have a right to be here are American citizens. For all others, their presence in the United States may be temporary or permanent. A person wishing to immigrate legally must first obtain a passport from his or her own country and apply for a visa from the U.S. State Department. A visa is a stamp or sticker placed in the passport that allows a person to proceed to one of over three hundred U.S. ports of entry. A visa allows a person to come *to* the United States, but only an immigration officer can actually authorize admission.

Applicants for entry can either be **immigrants** (people who intend to stay), or **non-immigrants** (people who come for a temporary purpose and intend to return to their home after a specified time). The requirements for non-immigrants are not as strict as the requirements for immigrants, so their processing is much faster.

A non-immigrant visa allows a person to stay in the United States to attend school, visit as a tourist, or be here for some other reason. Some visas allow for dual intent, that is, a person can use the non-immigrant visa for the stated purpose, and it may be used to obtain an immigrant visa at a later time. For persons holding visas that do not allow for dual intent, there is sometimes the possibility of "adjusting status." Bringing a fiancé into the country on a non-immigrant K-visa as a tourist, and later adjusting status to family reunification, is faster than trying to bring the fiancé in under the family reunification program as a spouse. (Either way, marriages must be legitimate. Immigration authorities have ways to detect bogus marriages.)

Immigrant Visas

Immigrant visas are the basis for "green cards," which are issued after a non-citizen has been legally admitted to the country. The first green card is good for two years; after that, they must be held for five years before applying for citizenship or updated every ten years. A **legal permanent resident (LPR)** is a non-citizen who holds a green card, and who is legally entitled to live and work in the United States. Green cards are a precursor for citizenship.

Family-sponsored reunification visas require that a U.S. citizen or legal permanent resident is able to prove a family relationship with the person seeking admission. Family reunification accounts for fifty percent or more immigrant visas issued each year. There are two basic categories for family-sponsored reunification, limited and unlimited, some with backlogs of ten to twelve years or longer.

Unlimited Visas

***Immediate Relative of a U.S. Citizen (IR)* visas** allows an adult U.S. citizen to petition for a spouse, parent(s), widow(er), or an unmarried child under the age of twenty-one, and apply for their relative's green card at the same time. IR visas can also be used for children adopted abroad.

***Returning Resident (SB)* visas** are for immigrants who previously lived in the United States and are returning after more than one year abroad.

Limited Visas

***F-1 First Preference* visas** admit unmarried adult children of U.S. citizens.

***F-2A Second Preference* visas** allow a Legal Permanent Resident (LPR) to petition for a spouse and any unmarried children over the age of twenty-one. This visa category is heavily backlogged.

***F-3 Third Preference* visas** admit married children of U.S. citizens.

***F-4 Fourth Preference* visas** admit siblings of adult U.S. citizens.

Diversity visas ("green card lottery") are available to a total of fifty-five thousand applicants from any country that has had fewer than fifty thousand immigrants admitted to the United States in the last five years. In 2011, a record fifteen million people applied for the random drawing. ... Most applicants are from Caribbean nations. Applicants must have a high school education and work experience. Winning applicants may also file for a spouse and any unmarried children under the age of twenty-one.

Employment-based visas require the sponsorship of an American employer and have varying levels of preference.

***First Preference EB-1* visas** are for priority workers, such as professors, researchers, athletes, or some other person with extraordinary skills.

***Second Preference EB-2* visas** are for persons holding advanced degrees or who have some exceptional ability. An EB-2 waiver may eliminate the need for a labor certification (LCA) required for many foreign workers by the U.S. Department of Labor (see H-1B non-immigrant visas).

***Third Preference EB-3* visas** are for skilled workers and other professionals.

***Fourth Preference EB-4* visas** are for religious workers, current or former government workers, and others. There are four specialized categories under the fourth preference, *SK-1* through *SK-4*.

Fifth Preference EB-5 **visas** involve trade treaties between two countries. For $500,000.00, an immigrant-investor can obtain a green card when his investment has produced ten new jobs for American workers (presuming that the applicant was in all other ways qualified for admission.

Special Immigrant **visas** are for interpreters from Iraq or Afghanistan, former employees in the Panama Canal Zone, Amerasians, and other persons in unique categories.

Sponsorship is a term used when there is no family relationship. The prospective sponsor(s) must undergo financial inspection of their finances in order to prove that they can provide for their own support, plus support at twenty-five percent above the poverty level for the immigrant for a period of ten years. Churches often sponsor immigrants under this category.

Non-Immigrant Visas

A-1 through A-3 visas are for foreign government officials, their families, and staff.

B visas are temporary visas for visitors. **B-1 visas** are for visitors on business. **B-2 visas** are for tourists and sometimes are used for persons seeking medical treatment.

C and D visas are "transit" visas for airline and ships crews.

E-1 and E-2 visas also involve treaties between two countries, but unlike EB-5 visas, they are non-immigrant visas.

F-1 through F-3 visas are for students attending an accredited college or university and their families. The number of foreign students decreased after 9-11. Employment is severely limited for students on F-1 visas.

G-1 through G-5 visas are for representatives of foreign governments, their families, and staff attending a meeting of an international organization.

H visas are temporary, specialized, non-immigrant work permits. They are not specific to country, but they are numerically restricted. The employer may be responsible for the worker's return transportation.

H-1A **visas** are for registered nurses.

H-1B visas generally require a college degree and a labor certification, which can take six months or longer. Labor certifications from the Department of Labor are based on a preference system that factors academic degrees, English language proficiency, and national security. One reason for this type of visa is that the United States does not graduate enough students in mathematics and sciences to fill the demand from American companies. Until 1990, there were no limits on H-1B visas. Once as high as 195,000, the limit is currently 65,000 per year. The limit is always exceeded on the first day of application. In addition to normal visa costs, the employer also has to pay $1,500.00 per employee.

H-2A visas are for seasonal agricultural work; **H-2B visas** are for temporary non-agricultural work. Neither can be used for temporarily filling a permanent job.

H-3 visas are for training purposes. They cannot be used to fill in for missing workers.

H-4 visas are for spouses and children in any of the other H categories.

Humanitarian Parole or "hardship" visas are limited to four thousand per year. Hardship visas are for applicants who do not qualify for any type of other visa consideration, but who present evidence of some pressing reason to enter the U.S., such as to attend a funeral.

I visas are for foreign journalists.

J-1 and J-2 visas are for educational exchange visitors and their families.

K-1 through K-4 visas are for spouses or fiancés of American citizens and their minor children. If a fiancé, the couple must marry within ninety days.

L-1 and L-2 visas are for intra-company transferees and their families. Degrees are not required. Visas are for one year at a time, up to a maximum of six years.

M-1 through M-3 visas are for students and their families at non-accredited schools, such as trade schools or Bible colleges.

N-8 and N-9 visas are for "special immigrants" of "certain international organizations," not specified.

NAFTA visas (See TN/TD visas.)

NATO 1 through NATO 7 visas are various visas for representatives of the North Atlantic Treaty Organization.

O-1 through O-3 visas are for persons with "extraordinary abilities," their families, and their support staff.

P-1 through P-4 visas are for athletes and entertainers and their families. They can be issued individually or as a group visa.

Q-1 through Q-3 visas are for cultural exchange visitors and their families.

R-1 and R-2 visas are for religious workers and their families.

S-5 through S-7, or "snitch" visas were created in 1994 to recruit informants in criminal or terrorism investigations.

T-1 through T-5 visas are for victims of trafficking in human cargo and their families. They are numerically limited, but they may be converted to Legal Permanent Resident status after three years.

Temporary Protected Status (TPS) visas can legally protect a person from certain troubled countries for eighteen months while awaiting adjudication of a visa application.

TN and TD visas ("NAFTA visas") generally require a college degree. These visas are only for Mexicans or Canadians and their families. Since 2008, they have been good for three years at a time.

TWOV visas are another form of transit visa (see also **C** and **D visas**).

U-1 through U-5 visas are for victims of "certain crimes," and their families. The crimes are generally sexual in nature. U visas are issued for four years at a time on the basis of cooperation with the prosecution, not on the verdict.

V-1 through V-3 visas involve family reunification applications made by relatives of Legal Permanent Residents, as opposed to U.S. citizens. It allows for temporary family reunification while the regular immigration process runs its course.

Refugees and Asylees

Refugees and persons seeking asylum ("asylees") are classified as humanitarian migrants. The United States enacted its first refugee law, The Displaced Persons Act (distinct from immigration laws) in 1948. However, from the post-WWII era to the post-Vietnam era, humanitarian admissions were episodic and haphazard. The U.S. experience with 130,000 refugees from Southeast Asia largely shaped the current law.[5]

The U.S. definition of a **refugee** conforms to the United Nations definition: a person outside of his homeland who is unable or unwilling to return to his home because of a well-founded fear of persecution based on race, religion, nationality, membership in a social group, or political opinion.[6] Refugees wanting to be admitted must undergo health screening, and may not have been convicted of any major crimes, although criminal records from many countries are virtually impossible to verify.

Asylees must meet the same criteria as refugees, but asylees are applicants applying for entry who are already physically here, legally or not.[7] Asylum is generally granted only for political purposes, and persons granted asylum in the United States are virtually always from a Communist country. A grant of asylum is for an initial period of one year.[8] After that, the asylum seeker may apply for a green card if conditions in the petitioner's home country have not improved.

Female genital mutilation (FGM) and homosexuality may qualify for refugee or asylee status. Cultural asylum (not an official category) may be offered to a woman from Senegal, Nigeria, Kenya, Ethiopia, Somalia, or some other country that practices female genital mutilation. A gay person from a country with extremely stringent prohibitions against homosexuality like Malaysia or Iran (where homosexuality demands the death penalty, even for minors) may successfully petition the U.S. government for refugee status.

Haitians and Dominicans picked up in open waters by the U.S. Coast Guard are returned to their home because they are deemed to be fleeing poor economic conditions, not Communism.[9] Many blacks in the United States claim this is racism because both groups are black, but the U.S. government views the interdiction of Haitians and Dominicans by the U.S. Coast Guard no differently than the border patrol apprehending Mexicans along the U.S.-Mexican border.

Cuban authorities complain that the United States is refusing to honor an agreement made in 1994 that was intended to allow twenty thousand Cuban citizens to emigrate yearly. The Cubans say that by issuing only half that number of visas, the United States is encouraging illegal migration.[10] Amnesty International and other groups have criticized U.S. asylum policy, saying that it is unmanageably broad, and allows would-be asylees to move to the head of the line in front of millions of legitimate immigrants.[11]

Notes

1 Daniel J. Tichenor, *Dividing Lines: The Politics of Immigration Control in America* (Princeton: Princeton UP, 2002), 48.

2 Tichenor, 53.

3 John F. Kennedy, "A Nation of Immigrants," *Immigration: Debating the Issues*, Ed. Nicholas Capaldi (Amherst: Prometheus, 1997), 124.

4 Gerald L. Neuman, *Strangers to the Constitution: Immigrants, Borders and Fundamental Law* (Princeton: Princeton UP, 1996), 125.

5 Roger Daniels, *Coming to America: A History of Immigration and Ethnicity in American Life*, 2nd ed. (New York: Perennial-HarperCollins, 2002), 345.

6 United States. U.S. Commission on Immigration Reform, *Refugee Policy* (Washington: GPO, 1997), 10, 11.

7 Daniels, *Coming to America*, 346.

8 *Refugee Policy*, 44, 52.

9 Daniels, *Coming to America*, 348.

10 Michelle Kelemen, "United States and Cuba Wrangle over Visas, Goods," *National Public Radio*, 10 Aug 2007 <http://www.NPR.org/templates/story.php?storyId=12668635>.

11 Dan Stein, Testimony of Dan Stein (FAIR) submitted to the Immigration Subcommittee of the Senate Judiciary Committee, 3 May 2001, 30 Jul 2009 <http://mnforsustain.org/steindasylumpolicyfair>.

Photo Credit: Pat Mcnulty www.premierphotographer.com

Chapter Three

CITIZENSHIP

> *A great test of a country is whether people are trying to get into it, or out of it.*
> Tony Blair[1]

Virtual Citizens

REFERRING TO UNDOCUMENTED persons in 2006, President Bush said, "[Illegal immigrants] are beyond the reach and protection of American law." The President was wrong. The Constitution applies to all persons within the geographical boundaries or territories of the United States.[2] The Bill of Rights protects citizens, legal permanent residents, visitors, refugees, asylum-seekers, and the undocumented alike.

Citizenship plays a minor role in the Constitution.[3] The Bill of Rights never uses the word citizen.[4] The Founding Fathers used the words "residents," "people," "persons," and "inhabitants. " In *Graham v. Richardson (1972)* the Supreme Court ruled that aliens (whom it called a "discrete and insular minority") were a group for whom special judicial protection is appropriate. Even undocumented persons enjoy virtually total rights because of the constitutional language, and legally settled non-citizens are virtual citizens. In *Pyler v Doe (1981)*, the U.S. Supreme Court ruled

> Whatever [a person's] status under the immigration laws, an alien is surely a "person" in any ordinary sense of that term. Aliens, even aliens whose presence in this country is unlawful, have long been recognized as persons guaranteed due process of law by the Fifth and Fourteenth Amendments. Indeed, we have clearly held that the Fifth Amendment protects aliens whose presence in this country is unlawful from invidious discrimination by the Federal Government.[5]

The wording of the Bill of Rights traces to Shays' Rebellion, 1786-1787.[6] Daniel Shays, a former captain in the Revolutionary Army, led a band of farmers, servants, free blacks, and laborers who were barred from citizenship, voting, and office holding, despite, in many cases, prior military service. Shays' Rebellion was quickly suppressed, but its message was remembered at the Constitutional Convention. Representatives worried about armed insurrection demanded that the Constitution contain a "bill of rights" that would restrict the government's power over the common people.

The Founders considered themselves to be citizens, and spelled out the rights of non-citizens in the language they used. The Founders could not have envisioned the importance of their work in today's immigration debate. Their language is subject to interpretation but unlikely to change.

U.S. citizenship does not grant any special advantage, or require much from those who have it.[7] Citizens benefit from the protections in the Bill of Rights, such as the freedoms of speech and religion, a free press, and the right to peaceful assembly. A citizen must obey laws and pay taxes. Non-citizens are expected to do likewise. Citizens may work, join, worship, attend, participate, and travel as they please. So may non-citizens.

The Bill of Rights guarantees specific rights to all persons in criminal proceedings, the right against unreasonable search and seizure, and the right to a writ of *habeas corpus*. In a criminal trial, it guarantees the right to an attorney, the rights against self-incrimination and double jeopardy, the right to a speedy and public trial, and protection against cruel and unusual punishment.

According to the Bureau of Alcohol, Tobacco, and Firearms, non-citizens may even own firearms, although it is doubtful they could get a permit to carry a concealed weapon in any state due to the legal concept of "no absolute right."[8]

Americans who do not approve of the Bill of Rights might consider a constitutional amendment to change some particular part of it. It only takes two thirds of the House and Senate to agree upon it, and only three quarters of the states to ratify a change.

"Anchor Babies"

Having a child born on U.S. soil does not produce an "anchor baby" for undocumented parents. A U.S. citizen child of undocumented parents has the same rights as any other U.S. citizen child, but children's rights are very limited and virtually no relief is available to undocumented parents. At best, when the U.S. citizen child reaches the age of majority (twenty one for immigration purposes in the U.S., as opposed to eighteen in Mexico), he can petition to sponsor his parents and siblings under the family reunification plan.[9]

This presumes that the family could remain undetected for twenty-one years, that the laws will not change adversely, and that the parents are prepared to hide for an additional ten years or more required for the family reunification to be approved, depending on their native country. Undocumented parents who get caught and find themselves in immigration court often protest, "You can't deport me. My child is a U.S. citizen." The judge's response will be, "I am deporting you because you broke the law. I'm not doing anything to your child."

Undocumented Children

Children carried across the border by undocumented parents are a different matter. These children had no say about coming here, did not knowingly, intentionally, or willfully commit an illegal act, and were powerless to prevent any illegal act committed by their parents. In *Pyler v Doe (1981)*, the U.S. Supreme Court struck down a Texas statute excluding undocumented children from public school attendance, and mandated K-12 education for all non-citizen children.[10]

> [The Texas statute] imposes a lifetime hardship on a discrete class of children not accountable for their disabling status. The stigma of illiteracy will mark them for the rest of their lives. By denying these children a basic education, we deny them the ability to live within the structure of our civic institutions, and foreclose any realistic possibility that they will contribute in even the smallest way to the progress of our Nation.[11]

The Dream Act

The mandate in *Pyler* does not apply to higher education.[12] Unfortunately, there is little incentive for undocumented students to excel in high school if they know they cannot pursue higher education, and their employment possibilities are limited due to the status conferred on them by their parents.[13] Very few undocumented children who do graduate from high school find a way to attend college. One exception is in Utah where undocumented students are not only allowed to attend public institutions of higher education, but they can receive in-state tuition as well.[14]

Proposed federal legislation, the "Dream Act" is meant to recognize that children who came here with their parents did not break any laws, and should not be considered illegal just because they are undocumented.

The Dream Act would allow applicants thirty-five years old or younger who entered the United States before their sixteenth birthday, who have no criminal record, and who have lived in this country for at least five years to be eligible for provisional citizenship upon graduation from high school. After completing two years of college or military service, these students would be allowed to petition for Legal Permanent Resident status, a precursor to citizenship. Proponents say that these young people look like us, talk like us, and have grown up pledging alliance to the flag and singing the Star Spangled Banner. For many, this is the only country they have ever known. Opponents of the bill (including some Hispanics) point out that students who are not academically gifted may not be the best candidates for military service if their enlistments are seen as punitive.

Senators Richard Durbin (D-Ill) and Richard Lugar (R-In) have been the leading sponsors of the Dream Act. During the Obama administration, removals of students have been indefinitely suspended so that Immigration and Customs Enforcement (ICE) can concentrate on "other priorities" (See Chapter Five). The Dream Act legislation was originally introduced in the senate in 2007, but was defeated by a filibuster. It was reintroduced in 2009 and defeated 55-41 in 2010.

Most states have restrictive legislation that bars applicants from achieving a college education. Utah, Texas, California, New York, Oklahoma, Illinois, Washington, Kansas and Nebraska have allowed some sort of admission conditions for undocumented students. A few other states have similar, but abbreviated, versions of educational benefits for undocumented students and as of early 2010, nine states have legislation that has been proposed.

California has its own version of the Dream Act, AB 131, passed in two parts and signed by Governor Jerry Brown in 2011. AB 131, which differs significantly from the proposed federal legislation, is scheduled to go into effect in January 2013 if it can withstand challenges from the right.

One obstacle is that many people think that a grant of in-state tuition is an extra expense to the taxpayer when the real issue is collecting in-state tuition or no tuition at all. Ultimately, the states have little incentive to go out on a limb without federal legislation which would legalize the status of the undocumented students.[15]

Routes to U.S. Citizenship

Jus Soli means "of the soil." This concept citizenship in the U.S. was established by the Fourteenth Amendment which states "all persons born or naturalized in the United States, and subject to the jurisdiction thereof, are citizens of the United States and of the state wherein they reside." Established in 1868 and later modified by statute, it was based on English Common Law. Its original function was granting citizenship to Negro males as a follow-up to the Emancipation Proclamation. At that time, the phrase "all persons" did not include Indians or women, and it has never included children born to foreign diplomats, children born on public vessels in U.S. coastal waters, or children born to women "accompanying an invading army."[16]

Any person born in the continental United States, Hawaii, Alaska, Puerto Rico, Guam, or the U.S. Virgin Islands is a U.S. citizen. A person born in American Samoa, the Northern Mariana Islands, or Swains Island is a "non-citizen national."[17] Many countries no longer use *jus soli*. It is contentious in the United States because it confers citizenship on children born here to undocumented parents, mainly Mexican.

Jus sanguineous, "of the blood," is parental or derivative citizenship. About fifty thousand children born abroad to American citizens, derive citizenship each year through this method.[18]

Combination Standard – The United States and other countries recognize both *jus soli* and *jus sanguineous*.

Naturalization – Although about 630,000 people are sworn in as American citizens each year, the United States does not actively promote naturalization, or only in a laissez-faire way at best.[19] The lack of official encouragement for naturalization may be part of the reason why millions of non-citizens who are eligible for citizenship do not pursue it.[20] The increased price for a citizenship application from $400.00 in 2007 to $675.00 in 2010 may be another reason. (Applicants for the previous step of becoming a legal permanent resident status (LPR) must pay $1,010.00, up from $395.00.)[21]

Another reason – which may come as a shock to most Americans – is that many migrants, especially Mexicans, do not intend to stay in the United States forever and do not want to become American citizens.[22] Xenophobes who fear that the national skin color of the United States will darken over the next fifty years should take some comfort in this.

The rate of naturalization for Mexican citizens was high between 1941 and 1945.[23] It was also higher than normal between 1995 and 2005, but Mexicans still have a comparatively low tendency to become U.S. citizens.[24] Canadians also have a very low rate of naturalization in the United States.

What is common to Mexico and Canada is that they both have a contiguous border with the United States.[25]

Favoring higher rates of naturalization, Harvard economist George Borjas has speculated that federal programs might be a potential magnet because usage of these programs goes up after an immigrant becomes a citizen.

Dr. Borjas did not define "federal programs," (the implication is that they are welfare) and he did not specify what this post-citizenship usage is. For skilled, English-fluent immigrants from India, for example, these programs might be grants or low interest college loans for their children, home loan assistance, disaster relief, or small business loans—programs available to all taxpayers, but not considered welfare. For the most part, Hispanics have relied on small business entrepreneurship, not legislation or government programs, for their economic success.

Applicants for naturalization must be free from health problems such as AIDS or tuberculosis, and deemed "unlikely to become a public charge." Applicants must also take an oath renouncing "any foreign prince, potentate, state, or sovereignty."[26] The United States is the only nation with language this strident in its oath.[27] Except in extreme cases like that of convicted Nazi prison guard John Demjanjuk, the U.S. government cannot take citizenship away. Generally, a person with U.S. citizenship must voluntarily relinquish it in order to lose it.

The difficulty of learning a new language is a recognized bar to citizenship worldwide, and many migrants feel that English is too difficult to learn.[28] Other migrants do not apply for citizenship for fear that the naturalization process might cause them to suffer financial loss in their native country, such as the loss of real property or being left out of a will.[29]

Adoption – Adopting a child from a foreign country, or adopting the child of a non-citizen spouse, confers instant citizenship on the child.[30] The government charges $700.00 to recognize this, up from $545.00.

Private Bills by Congress – Seeking congressional support for special circumstances is usually politically motivated, and generally fails.

Parental Naturalization – Children under the age of fourteen are automatically naturalized when a parent is naturalized.[31] These children cannot decline U.S. citizenship, although they can renounce it when they reach the age of twenty-one.

Unique Circumstances – Article VIII of the Treaty of Guadalupe Hidalgo of 1852 gave border residents one year to choose between U.S. and Mexican citizenship. After one year, U.S. citizenship was deemed to have been elected by those who were non-declarant.[32]

Honorary citizenship to "uniquely qualified individuals" – So far, only Winston Churchill and Mother Teresa have been so honored

* * *

U.S. citizenship is generally determined through the father's line, although this has been contested many times over the years. In the case of unwed parents, citizenship is determined through the mother's line.[33]

Dual citizenship is not the same as multiple citizenships. Dual citizenship occurs at the moment of birth and is not chosen. The number of Americans holding dual citizenship is in the millions.[34] Unlike naturalization, the United States does not require dual citizens to choose one nationality over another.[35]

An (extreme) example of multiple citizenships would be a child born on U.S. soil of a father holding dual citizenship in countries A and B, and a mother holding dual citizenship in countries C and D. The child would be a citizen of the United States by the principle of *jus soli*. Subject to probable restrictions, the child might also be able to claim citizenship in countries A, B, C, and D by the principle of *jus sanguineous*.[36] On the other hand, a child born in a *jus sanguineous* country to parents who are citizens of a *jus soli* country would have *no* citizenship until the parents adopted their own child.[37]

In the future, the 1993 European Union's Maastricht Treaty will likely present new challenges to understandings of citizenship.

Notes

1 Tony Blair, *Late Night with David Letterman*, prod./dir. Jerry Foley, CBS, 8 September 2009.

2 T. Alexander Aleinikoff, "Between Principles and Politics: U.S. Citizenship Policy," *From Migrants to Citizens: Membership in a Changing World*, Eds. T. Alexander Aleinikoff and Douglas Klusmeyer (Washington: Carnegie Endowment for International Peace, 2000), 156.

3 Aleinikoff, "Between Principles," 151.

4 Aleinikoff, "Between Principles," 150.

5 Pyler v. Doe, 457 United States 202, 102 S. Ct. 2382, 72 Led. 2d 786, 1982.

6 Richard Shenkman, *I Love Paul Revere Whether He Rode or Not* (New York: HarperCollins, 1991), 80, 81.

7 Peter H. Shuck, "Membership in the Liberal Polity," *Immigration and Refugee Law and Policy*, 3rd ed., Ed. Stephen H. Legomsky (New York: Foundation Press, 1997), 1183.

8 If permission to carry a concealed firearm was not tattooed on the bottom of your foot while you were in the womb, or if your name is not specifically mentioned in the Constitution, you probably have "no absolute right."

9 Gerald L. Neuman, *Strangers to the Constitution: Immigrants, Borders and Fundamental Law* (Princeton: Princeton UP, 1996), 181,182.

10 Aleinikoff, "Between Principles," 153.

11 Aleinikoff, "Between Principles," 153.

12 Aleinikoff, "Between Principles," 152.

13 Aleinikoff, "Between Principles," (quoting Peter Shuck), 128.

14 Haya El Nasser, "Immigrants Turn Utah into Mini-Melting Pot," *USA Today*, 15 Sep 06: 1A.

15 William Perez, *We are Americans: Undocumented Students Pursuing the American Dream* (Sterling: Stylus, 2009), *xxvii-xxix*. Perez may be the only author writing about this facet of the immigration debate.

16 Neuman, *Strangers*, 165.

17 Stephen H. Legomsky, *Immigration and Refugee Law and Policy*, 3rd ed. (New York: Foundation Press, 2002), 1169, 1170.

18 Aleinikoff, "Between Principles," 129.

19 Klusmeyer, Introduction, *Migrants*, 16.

20 Klusmeyer, Introduction, *Migrants*, 16.

21 Julia Preston, "United States Raising Visa Fees 66% on Average, to Advocates Dismay," *New York Times*, 30 May 2007 <http://www.nytimes.com/Washington/fees>. Prices quoted in this chapter are taken from this article. They may have already changed.

22 Sam Quinones, *True Tales from Another Mexico: The Lynch Mob, the Popsicle Kings, Chalino, and the Bronx* (Albuquerque: New Mexico UP, 2001), 292.

23 Elliot Robert Barkan, *And Still They Come: Immigrants and American Society 1920 to the 1990s*, Eds. John Hope Franklin and A. S. Eisenstadt (Wheeling: Harlan Davidson, 1996), 67, The American History Series.

24 Jeffrey S. Passel, "Growing Share of Immigrants Choosing Naturalization," Pew Hispanic Center, 27 Sep 2005, 28 Mar 2007 <http://pewhispanic.org/reports/report.php?ReportID=74>.

25 Barkan, *And Still They Come*, 106.

26 Aleinikoff, "Between Principles," 130.

27 David A. Martin, Introduction, *Migrants*, 27.

28 Klusmeyer, Introduction, *Migrants*, 17, 18.

29 Aleinikoff, "Between Principles," 131.

30 Klusmeyer, Introduction, *Migrants*, 5.

31 Klusmeyer.

32 Richard Griswold del Castillo, *The Treaty of Guadalupe Hidalgo: A Legacy of Conflict* (Norman: Oklahoma UP, 1990), 66-72.

33 Legomsky, *Immigration*, 1200, 1202.

34 Miriam Feldblum, "Managing Membership: New Trends in Citizenship and Nationality Policy," *Migrants*, 478.

35 Aleinikoff, "Between Principles," 147.

36 Aleinikoff, "Between Principles," 140.

37 Legomsky, *Immigration*, 1222

Chapter Four

POPULATION AND SOCIAL SECURITY

> *Immigration has never been relatively higher than when the second Pilgrim came down the gangplank, increasing the Plymouth Colony population by 100 %.*
> Peter Brimelow[1]

Migrants

MIGRATION IS ALMOST purely economic in nature, so it is important to understand that migrants come here to work, but may leave when there is no work. In 1998, the Mexican Secretariat for Foreign Relations estimated that sixty-five percent of all Mexican migrants, legal or illegal, returned to Mexico within ten years, taking with them small American consumer goods, automobiles, and new skills for the Mexican workplace.[2]

The migration rate for legal migration is expressed as them/us. If there were 100 migrants, and the host population numbered 1000, the formula would be 100/1000, or 10 percent. At mid-year 2005, the foreign-born population was 12.1 percent.[3] That was up two percent from the 2000 Census, but lower than the all time high of 13.2 percent in 1920.[4]

The method for determining the size of the illegal population is always an estimate. It involves taking the legal immigrant population and subtracting it from the number of foreign-born residents. The remainder is thought to be the number of illegal migrants; until recently, about twelve million, with Hispanics the majority of that cohort.

It is necessary to distinguish between raw numbers and percentages, and to keep everything in context. For instance, illegal migration would appear to be dwarfed by the number of abortions performed in the United States each year.[5]

The Census Bureau projected that the Hispanic population would account for forty-four percent of the nation's growth (not population) from 2000 to 2020, and sixty-two percent of growth from 2020 to 2050. The 2010 Census indicated that Hispanics accounted for fifty percent of the population growth in the last decade.[6] By some estimates, the U.S. Hispanic population could reach 96.5 million by the middle of this century.[7] However, the current projections for 2000 to 2020 may be high because the demographers could not have predicted the worldwide recession in 2008, and the presumed decline in the birth rate and in-migration, plus whatever out-migration that might have accompanied it.

The public only hears about people who come here, but the U.S. government does not have any mechanism for counting people who leave, whether temporarily or permanently. Figures for out-migration must be assembled from various indicators. History offers some examples.

Some industries that employed large numbers of Mexican migrants during World War I paid their return transportation home in the early 1920s. The Ford Motor Company paid for the repatriation of 3,000 of its Mexican workers.[8] The crash of the Stock Market and the Great Depression halted and reversed Mexican migration.[9] Between 400,000 to 600,000 Hispanics left the United States, some at gunpoint, during the 1930s.[10] As many as half of them may have been U.S. citizens.[11] During the twenty-two years of the *Bracero* Program, millions of illegal workers were apprehended and sent back to Mexico. At the conclusion of the *Bracero* Program in 1964, millions of *braceros* were deported to Mexico. During Operation Wetback, 1954-1955, 1.25 million Mexicans were forcibly repatriated.[12]

During the period 1966 to 1993, approximately 3.5 million migrants left the United States, or about twenty percent of the number who came during the same period.[13] In 2004 alone, the Bureau of Immigration and Customs Enforcement (ICE) removed 202,842 foreign nationals, seventy-three percent of whom were Mexican. More than 1,035,000 other foreign nationals accepted what ICE refers to as "voluntary departure," and the Department of Homeland Security removed another 88,897 criminal aliens from the United States, seventy-seven percent of whom were Mexican. Altogether, 1,241,089 *indocumentados* were prevented from entering the country and 1,326,739 foreign nationals were removed from the country in that one year.[14]

In 2009, under the Obama administration, ICE deported 389,834 undocumented people, 20,000 more than in 2008 under George Bush. About half of this number had criminal records, in line with the administration's decision to target migrants with criminal records.[15] Unfortunately, these figures do not sell newspapers.

Boomers

There are many reasons for the current level of migration. From 1946 to 1964 the United States experienced a fifteen-year population explosion known as the "baby boom," which was accomplished almost entirely by natural increase. Americans who survived the great depression, World War II, or the Korean Conflict wanted to live a good life, enjoy material possessions, have big families, and provide for their children in ways that they themselves did not enjoy.

Government programs drove postwar growth in the private and public sector. Higher education became available on a large scale for the first time, and former servicemen took advantage of GI Bill educational benefits. Low cost VA home loans spurred the home construction industry. The Cold War and the threat of Communism kept the military large, and created more than enough jobs to go around.

Against this backdrop in 1968, a UCLA professor, Dr. Paul Erlich, wrote *The Population Bomb*. Erlich proposed that a luxury tax be placed on layettes, cribs, diapers, and diaper services.[16] Unfortunately, the people that professor Erlich needed to reach probably could not read or were heavily influenced by the Catholic Church. Visionaries don't always have good vision.

"Doomster" theory has been around since Robert Thomas Malthus first voiced it in the mid-1800s.[17] Professor Erlich's book convinced the United States and other first world countries to take immediate and severe action. Given doomsday scenarios at every turn, Planned Parenthood and other players got in the act during the next twenty years. Citizens of western nations stopped procreating, but did so too quickly. In the U.S., zero population growth (ZPG) went from being a catch phrase to a reality. Fertility rates dropped from a record twentieth century high of 3.8 in 1957 to just over the replacement rate, a measure where couples have just enough children to replace themselves (about 2.1 children per couple, after infant mortality is factored in).[18] The record low replacement rate was 1.7 in 1977.[19] America's fertility rate did not climb back to the 2.1 replacement rate again until 2006.[20] In 2011, it was 2.06.[21]

In Mexico, the fertility rate dropped from 6.8 in 1960 to 2.31 in 2011.[22] This will have the effect of drastically lowering the potential supply of migrant workers, something the anti-immigration lobbies have not considered.

In the United States, several conjoined factors led to rapid population decline. The first was that baby boomers grew up believing that they would not be able to live as well as their parents. The second factor was an intense and sustained consumer campaign that convinced the boomers to buy things that they did not need and could not afford. Not having children became the only way that allowed the boomers to have the consumer goods they wanted.

The United States has experienced a declining natural population nearly every year since the introduction of the birth control pill in 1960 and *Roe v. Wade* in 1973. (Ironically, the pill came from research designed to promote fertility.) Also, the women's rights movement promoted the idea that women were more than their reproductive capacity, and as educational opportunities for women went up, family size went down.[23]

Erlich, consumerism, birth control, and the women's movement went hand in hand in hand in hand.

The Doomsters who think that the U.S. is overpopulating should consider the following: there are 266,807 square miles in the state of Texas. Subtracting two percent for federally owned land and railroad right-of-way leaves 261,471 square miles. Multiplying 640 acres per square mile yields 167,341,440 acres in Texas. Divided by the U.S. population of approximately 311 million people – young and old, male and female, gay and straight, legal and illegal, red and yellow black and white – every person would have a half acre to live on (.5381 acres per person) with plenty left over for streets and shopping malls, churches and schools. These calculations yield a half acre for every person, not every family. If that is not good enough, do the math for Alaska.

One last thing must be factored in. After the precipitous drop in the birth rate, what few children the boomers did have, "had" to go to college, or so their boomer parents told them. Currently, thirty percent of the U.S. workforce (not the population) has a college education. Now there is a serious shortage of blue-collar workers.[24]

Under populating created a situation ripe for increased migration. At the end of the twentieth century, migration accounted for more than a third of the population increase in the United States.[25] By 2006, it accounted for forty percent of population growth.[26] The birth rate of migrant women in the U.S. is initially similar to that in their native country, but their fertility tends to approximate that of the host country after a generation or two.[27]

Social Security and the Graying of America

Photo Credit: Vincent Blaine

Social Security

When President Roosevelt established the Old Age Assistance program in 1935 it was not meant become a retirement income for every citizen, and the retirement age of sixty-five was chosen because not many people were likely to reach it, or live long afterward if they did.[28]

In 1983, Congress created the Social Security Trust Fund, which was intended to insure the stability of Social Security against shortfalls. The fund has shown surpluses every year since, but much of that money is on loan to other government agencies.

The Social Security Administration's *suspense* fund always contains tens of billions of dollars – perhaps hundreds of billions of dollars — in wage deductions that can not be matched to any Social Security number. The agency's inspector general told Congress that undocumented workers who will never realize any benefits from their contributions are the source of most of that money.[29] The National Academy of Sciences has estimated that the overall value of migrants to the economy is approximately $30 billion dollars per year.[30]

In a classic example of one hand not knowing–or caring–what the other hand is doing, projections from the Social Security Administration anticipate that migrants will continue contributing, but the Department of Homeland Security will continue trying to keep them out.

* * *

An unfavorable age distribution, or imbalance – sometimes called "the graying of America"– is a problem the United States has never faced before. More people will need medical or social support, but there will be fewer people to support them, or carry on the work of the nation. In addition to its impact on Social Security, this has implications for education, politics, national defense, taxes, pension plans, and many other aspects of American life. Thanks to the baby boomers (actually their parents), America has a growing senior population but a shrinking taxpayer base. The U.S. may soon have more grandparents than grandchildren.

At mid-decade, there were approximately 302 million people in the United States.[31] Seventy-four million of them were under the age of eighteen, or 24 percent of the population. There were thirty-eight million seniors, or thirteen percent of the population. This combined 115 million people, or thirty-eight percent of the population, is referred to as the dependent population.[32]

Subtracting the dependent population from the total population left a potential workforce aged eighteen to sixty-four of 187 million people, or sixty-two percent of the population. However, not all of those people were actually employed because of health or disability, educational status, incarceration, military service, or choice.

What is not immediately seen on the surface is that seventy-eight million of the people in that workforce—nearly forty-one percent of them—are baby boomers who began reaching full retirement age in record numbers beginning in 2011. The dependency ratio will continue to worsen for fifteen years, corresponding to the length of the baby boom.

More retirees not only means more seniors drawing Social Security, but advances in medical technology will mean that this population will live longer, on the average 77.4 years, although not all of them will be productive. The Census Bureau estimates that the number of centenarians will jump from 80,000 currently to 581,000 by 2040.[33]

In addition to the rapidly growing senior population, the country also has a declining population of young people, which means a shrinking tax base. In the 1960s, there were nearly four people working for every person who was not working.[34] In 2006, there were three people working for every two people not working. By 2030, the ratio of workers to beneficiaries is predicted to be 2:1, but it could reach that level sooner than predicted.[35]

Americans cannot envision living with high, European-style taxes that would be required to support Social Security, Medicare, and other government programs at their current levels, but Americans have also done little to prevent this.

Short-term fixes are popular in the House of Representatives where members stand for reelection every two years. Hard choices for Congress would be raising taxes, lowering benefits, finding new ways to fund Social Security, or making saving more attractive (most boomers have saved little and will not save when interest rates are low). Spain and Russia have made having more babies lucrative, offering $3,200.00 to $9,000.00 respectively for second or third children.

Average wage earners are taxed on everything they earn, but not the well-to-do, whose Social Security contributions end after their first $107,000.00 of yearly earnings. One possibility would be to employ an affluence test to eliminate well-to-do seniors from all benefits, giving them back what they have paid in with interest, but no more.

The U.S. is already forcing later retirement, and each year that retirement is moved forward is one more year of payroll contributions coming in. Also, the retirement of older workers will open up jobs for younger workers, which might be welcomed even if the younger workers had to pay higher taxes in order to support their parent's generation.

There will be a positive side to this transitional period. There will be increased employment in all areas of health care, and many new entrepreneurial opportunities relative to the senior market.

Birth and death rates do not change quickly. The problems associated with population decline will not only last through the fifteen-year period corresponding to the baby boom, but through the next generation if the boomer's children are not particularly fecund.

Migration is more flexible than birth and death rates. Adding migrant workers to the economy will expand the tax base, raise the gross national product, and lower the dependency ratios. Further, natural increase requires eighteen years to produce a taxpayer. In the category of extra added benefit, the expense of raising and educating the migrant taxpayers will have been borne by someone else.[36]

The frequently heard argument that migrants do not pay taxes is sometimes true, sometimes not true. It is true that newly arrived migrants will not pay as much tax as American workers because they will not initially earn as much. Unfortunately, some employers take deductions from the paychecks of undocumented employees, but do not pay them into the system. The migrant may think he is paying taxes, when he is not. If the migrant does not have legal status, he is not in a position to complain when the employer pockets the money. Self-employment by migrants can also be a problem as it can be with native-born workers. Increased migration will only work when all workers are legal and taxes are not only taken out of the employee's pay, but paid into the federal government (see Chapter 10).

Few migrants own their own home, but they all pay property tax as a portion of rent, and all migrants pay sales tax. Also, most migrants are young and will not have elderly parents living here who are drawing Social Security or other benefits.

However, this scenario can go on for just so long. A situation where young, uneducated Hispanics find themselves supporting well-educated, retired Americans for any length of time will be seen as both exploitive and racist. These workers will not tolerate having their paychecks eaten up by high taxes to fund Social Security benefits for native-born seniors, while having no hope of ever receiving those benefits themselves.

* * *

The subject of Social Security does hold one surprise for most Americans. A person does not have to be a U.S. citizen to draw Social Security, which is an earned benefit, and they don't have to live here to collect those benefits. Non-citizens who have worked legally in the United States and had Social Security deductions taken from their wages for the required length of time (approximately ten years) can move to another country and have their Social Security check mailed to them.[37] Social Security is like money in a bank. When it is time to withdraw the money, the citizenship and the mailing address of the account holder are of no concern to the bank. Likewise, they are of no concern to the Social Security Administration.

Notes

1 Peter Brimelow, "Time to Rethink Immigration," *Immigration: Debating the Issues,* Ed. Nicholas Capaldi (Amherst: Prometheus, 1997), 36.

2 Manuel Becerra Ramirez, "Nationality in Mexico," *From Migrants to Citizens: Membership in a Changing World,* Eds. Alexander Aleinikoff and Douglas Klusmeyer (Washington: Carnegie Endowment for International Peace, 2000), 331. (Ramirez cites *Reforma,* 1998, 2A).

3 United States. U.S. Census Bureau, U.S. Census Bureau Press Release (Washington: GPO, 2006).

4 Peter H. Shuck, "Alien Rumination" *Immigration and Refugee Law and Policy,* 3rd ed., Ed. Stephen H. Legomsky (New York: Foundation Press, 1997), 67.

5 "Abortion in the United States: Statistics and Trends," National Right to Life, 20 Oct 2004 and other years. Statistics from the Alan Guttmacher Institute, a research affiliate of Planned Parenthood, reveal a higher number of abortions than the Centers for Disease Control. However, both figures are lower than the actual figure because Guttmacher and the CDC only count documented, legal abortions, 20 Oct 2004, 29 Jan 2007 < http://www.nrlc.org/abortion/facts/abortionistats.html>.

6 "Census: Hispanics now Comprise 1 in 6 Americans," <http://www.cbsnews.com/stories/2011/03/24/m\national/main...3/24/11>.

7 United States. U.S. Census Bureau, "Helping You Make Informed Decisions" (Washington, GPO: undated pamphlet).

8 Matt A. Meier and Feliciano Ribera, *Mexican Americans/American Mexicans: from Conquistadors to Chicanos* (New York: Hill and Wang-Farrar Straus & Giroux, 1972), 124, 125.

9 Meier, *Mexican Americans,* 127.

10 Wesley Koch, "United States Urged to Apologize for 1930s Deportations," *USA Today,* 5 Apr 2006: 1A-2A.

11 Elliot Robert Barkan, *And Still They Come: Immigrants and American Society 1920 to the 1990s,* Eds. John Hope Franklin and A. S. Eisenstadt (Wheeling: Harlan Davidson, 1996), 47. The American History Series.

12 Barkan, *And Still They Come*, 84.

13 Barkan, *And Still they Come*, 123.

14 United States. U.S. Department of Homeland Security Management Directive, *Immigration Enforcement Actions: 2004* by Mary Dougherty, Denise Wilson and Amy Wu (Washington: GPO, 2005), 1.

15 Julia Preston, Students Spared Amid an Increase in Deportations, *New York Times*, 9 August 2010, 17 August 2010 <http://www.nytimes.com/2020/08/09/us/09students>.

16 Paul R. Erlich, *The Population Bomb* (New York: Ballentine, 1970), 137.

17 Malthus believed that population grows geometrically, while the means of subsistence increases arithmetically. Believers in Malthusian philosophy are called "doomsters." Those who believe that man is able to solve his problems through common sense, common interest, and technology are called "boomsters."

18 "United States Fertility Trends: Boom and Bust and Leveling Off," Ameristat Population Reference Bureau, 2003 29, Jan 2007 <http://www.prb.org/AmeristatTemplate.cfm?Section=Fertility>.

19 Haya El Nasser and Paul Overberg, "Fertility Rate in USA on Upswing," *USA Today*, 19 Dec 2007, 20 Dec 2007 <http://www.usatoday.com/news/nation>.

20 Peter G. Peterson, *Gray Dawn: How the Coming Age Wave Will Transform America and the World* (New York: Three Rivers-Random House, 2000), 48.

21 United States. Central Intelligence Agency, CIA World-Factbook, Mexico (Washington, GPO: 2011) <https://www.cia.gov/libraries/publications/world-factbook/geos/mx/html>.

22 Peterson, *Gray Dawn*, 48.

23 John R. Weeks, *Population* (Belmont: Wadsworth, 1999), 196-197.

24 United States. U.S. Census Bureau Press Release (Washington: GPO, 2006).

25 Weeks, *Population*, 25.

26 "The Main Event," *Wall Street Journal* 20/21 Oct 2006: A 7.

27 Weeks, *Population*, 387.

28 Peterson, *Gray Dawn*, 40.

29 Kathy Kiely, "Social Security, Immigration Entwined in Debate," *USA Today*, Jun 2007: 5A.

30 "Immigration Heritage," Review and Outlook, *Wall Street Journal*, 30 Jun 2007: A 16.

31 United States. U.S. Census Bureau, 2005-2007 American Community Survey Three Year Estimates. 16 Apr 2009, 10 Jun 2009 <http://factfinder.census.gov>. The 302 million comes from Table GCT-T1-R, "2007 Population Estimates." Obviously, the population has increased since this report. As of mid-year 2011, the United States population was estimated to be 311 million.

32 The figures given are projections for 2008, based on estimates from 2006. Calculations for dependent populations are not uniform between demographers, and the Census Bureau and the Social Security Administration do not always agree. Some demographers use fifteen to seventeen years of age for the lower end, while some use sixty-five to sixty-seven years of age at the upper end. Changing the upper range is understandable since the age for full retirement is being incrementally advanced from sixty-five to seventy by the Social Security Administration, but one would be hard pressed to find any fifteen year olds Americans who were self-supporting.

33 "Washington Wire," *Wall Street Journal*, 4 May 2007: A6.

34 Weeks, *Population*, 339.

35 *Wall Street Journal* "The United States: 300 Million Are Coming," 20/21 Oct 2006: A-7.

36 Peterson, *Gray Dawn*, 102.

37 Brian Grow, "Embracing Illegals: Companies Are Getting Hooked on the Buying Power of 11 Million Undocumented Immigrants," *Business Week*, 18 Jul 2005: 59.

Photo Credit: Vincent Blaine

Chapter Five

CRIME

> *Despite the public perception that Hispanic communities are riddled with crime, studies show the involvement of Hispanics in crime is less than that of the U.S.*[1]

Statistical Problems with Reporting Hispanic Crime

A NUMBER OF caveats must be observed for any discussion of Hispanic crime. This chapter was compiled using the best data available. However, the same type of data is not always available for comparison, or has not been processed in the same way for all timeframes, and the focus of similar studies is not always exactly the same. The correct use of terminology is also critical. For example, for one agency the term "legal status" may refer to a person's status as documented or undocumented, but for the Bureau of Prisons it means awaiting trial versus convicted.

"All prisoners confined to state or federal prisons or in city or county jails" is not the same as "all prisoners" if it does not include secure and non-secure privately-operated prisons, juvenile facilities, facilities for the criminally insane, military correctional facilities, forestry work crews or similar programs, tribal jails, Immigration and Customs Enforcement (ICE) facilities, and prisoners sentenced and confined by the District of Columbia Superior Court system.

Some prisoners with sentences of less than one year may not be confined in the traditional sense, but could be under alternative sentencing such as community service, home confinement, electronic monitoring, work release, or weekend reporting. Also, there is a difference between being under the jurisdiction of a level of government and being in the custody of that government, such as an inmate being temporarily held in a county jail on a federal charge.

Language, race and ethnicity can also be problematic. The term "Hispanic" is a language-based term. It is based on self-description, but since 2000, the U.S. Census Bureau has allowed respondents to choose more than one race in defining themselves (refer to Chapter One). In determining ethnicity, a person's native language is of no interest to the Bureau of Prisons, although it is the primary determinant of ethnicity for the U.S. Census Bureau. Also, law enforcement agencies report crime by sex and race, but not on the language spoken by the alleged perpetrator.

The federal Office of Management and Budget (OMB) standardizes the collection language of all agencies that fall under it, but outside agencies may use different standards, such as counting Hispanics as Caucasian, which is technically correct. However, this practice results in overstating the number of white prisoners, and understating the number of Hispanic prisoners.[2]

Also, care must be taken in comparing criminal statistics for migrants in different time periods. Incarceration figures are influenced by varying rates of migrant flow from year to year, increased or decreased levels of border enforcement, changes in underage populations, parole violations, and sentencing standards mandated by the federal court system, such as the "three strikes" rule. Between 1985 and 1990, time served for immigration offenses increased six-fold, due solely to changes in sentencing standards.

It is easy to get confused. In his book, *State of Emergency*, Patrick Buchanan stated that "thirty-nine percent of prisoners in Federal Bureau of Prison facilities" were non-citizens, whom he referred to as "criminal aliens."[3] Actually, only nineteen percent of the prisoners held in federal facilities were non-citizens, not thirty-nine percent. The thirty-nine percent figure is that of all non-citizens in both federal *and* state facilities, sixty-one percent were in state facilities while thirty-nine percent of them were in the federal system.[4] These non-citizens could have been of any race or nationality. Hispanics, whom Mr. Buchanan frequently rails about, were a sizeable part of but not all of the non-citizen total.

There are huge differences in reporting criteria, research methodologies and internal agency requirements. Some reports are dated at mid-year, others at year-end. Some studies take years to produce and may appear dated when they are actually the most recent information available.

Hispanic Crime – General

There are four categories of crime involving Hispanics. The first is crime by Hispanics against members of the native population. U.S. citizens worry about this. Second is crime against Hispanics by the members of the native population. Newly arrived Hispanics are visible targets, they carry cash, and they are unlikely to call the police. The third category is crime by Hispanics against other Hispanics. No one pays much attention to that. Finally, there are immigration offenses, which are civil, not criminal, offenses.

From California's Proposition 187 in 1994 (overturned) to Hazelton, Pennsylvania's, attempt at municipal control of migration (declared void), undocumented migrants are blamed for much crime that is not their doing.[5] Most anti-immigrant legislation cites the danger of fictitious crime in states that don't have an immigration problem. Alabama, Arizona, Georgia, Indiana, Oklahoma, South Carolina and Utah have passed anti-illegal immigration measures. Of these, only Arizona is a border state.

A pattern has emerged as to how these laws are being interpreted at the federal level suggesting that it is unconstitutional for states to try to enforce federal immigration laws. A challenge to Alabama's laws will probably be the first to be heard by the U.S. Supreme Court.

In November 2007, the *Congressional Quarterly* published its list of America's ten safest cities with populations of 500,000 or more. Four were in Texas—Fort Worth, San Antonio, Austin, and El Paso. Notably, crime was down thirty-six percent in El Paso, at that time the second safest city on the list despite its proximity to Juarez, Mexico. In California, San Jose and San Diego made the list. What these cities have in common are their migrant-rich populations and their proximity to the U.S.-Mexican border.[6]

For the decade between 1995 and 2005, U.S. Department of Justice Statistics indicated that violent crime declined thirty-four percent overall, homicides fell thirty-eight percent, assaults dropped thirty-two percent, robberies fell forty-one percent, and property crimes dropped twenty-six percent. The rate of illegal migration doubled during the same period.[7] If increased migration is associated with increased crime, crime should have gone up, but just the opposite was true—as migration went up, crime went down. Studies dating back to the Dillingham Report in 1901 exhibit the same pattern.[8]

Foreign-born Mexican men comprise one-third of all foreign-born men between the ages of eighteen and thirty-nine, they have the lowest levels of education of any ethnic group, and they account for the majority of illegal immigrants.[9] Conventional wisdom would predict high rates of incarceration, but the opposite is the case.[10] Crime rates are not a product of a person's nativity or immigration status.[11]

First-generation migrants are not responsible for much crime. They had the intelligence to recognize a bad situation that was unlikely to improve in their native country, and they had the initiative and courage to travel thousands of miles to an uncertain future in a country where they probably did not speak the language. The first generation of any ethnic group is oriented toward working long hours, and compared to what they left behind, most are comfortable in their comparatively luxurious surroundings. They may have hoped for a swimming pool, but at least they got a flush toilet. Their incentive to commit crime is low.

With all ethnic groups, the propensity toward crime increases in the second generation.[12] U.S. born Hispanics are seven times more likely to be in prison than their foreign-born counterparts.[13] Members of this cohort are U.S. citizens, products of the American educational system, American television, and American consumerism. Many are not satisfied with their parents' way of life because they have seen better.

Incarceration of Hispanics

With all these variables in mind, there were 2,293,157 persons in some form of custody in the United States on December 31, 2007.[14] State and federal prisons accounted for 1,512,576 inmates, or two-thirds of the nation's incarcerated population.[15] The remaining third, 780,581 inmates, were under local custody, sometimes in alternate sentencing programs.[16]

In the state and federal system at year-end 2007, the race or ethnicity of prisoners was eighteen percent Hispanic, thirty-one percent Caucasian, and thirty-six percent black.[17] Viewed as a percentage of their populations, the numbers are consistent.

The most recent study of the federal prison population comparing crime to race or ethnicity is from year-end 2007. Some change is to be expected, but general patterns are probably consistent. Thirty-five percent, or 45,756 of the prisoners in this study were non-citizen males. Of these non-citizens, eighty-one percent, or 37,062 prisoners were non-citizen Hispanics.[18] However, this group comprised only eighteen percent of the total federal prison population.[19]

The breakdown of these Hispanic males by offense type was as follows: violent offenses, 998; weapon offenses, 2,668; property offenses, 1,135; and drug offenses, 30,417. Immigration charges accounted for 18,117 offenders.[20] The total for these offenses, 53,335, was greater than the total of Hispanic prisoners (37,062) because many of the prisoners were held on multiple charges.

However, many prisoners held on immigration charges were never arrested, charged, tried, found guilty, or sentenced for anything other than the immigration crime. Immigration charges include unlawful entry or reentry, smuggling, transporting, harboring, and misuse of official documents. The most common immigration offense is illegal entry, and most offenders are Mexicans males under the age of thirty. Offenders charged with reentry tend to be older and many have prior felony convictions.

Prisoners held on immigration offenses are not entitled to a public defender and most do not have money to hire private counsel. They typically serve the longest sentences.

Capital Crimes by Hispanics

Of all prisoners executed since the U.S. Supreme Court reinstated the death penalty in 1977, fifty-seven percent were white, thirty-four percent were black, seven percent were Hispanic, and two percent were "other races."[21] Through 2008, there were only thirteen executions of Hispanic prisoners, three in 2004, three in 2005, two in 2006, three in 2007, and two in 2008.[22] In 2009 there were six executions of Hispanic prisoners, all in Texas.[23] Texas executed five Hispanics in 2010 and four in 2011. Florida executed one Hispanic in 2011. Some of these men were U.S. citizens, some may have held dual citizenship, some were foreign nationals. Critics of Mexican migration say that there would be more executions of Hispanics if Mexico would extradite its citizens to the United States for capital cases. Mexican President Felipe Calderon has begun extraditing drug lords to the United States for non-capital offenses, but Mexico is one of many countries that will not extradite to the United States when the death penalty could be involved.

Legal Responses

Many state and local law enforcement officials feel that it is not their job to enforce immigration laws. Additionally, they cite the lack of time and resources. This situation is similar to 1982 when the former Immigration and Naturalization Service (INS) requested that educational institutions keep track of foreign students instead of the federal government doing it. The idea of a federal agency shifting its workload to private or state institutions did not sit well with Congress, although it was suggested again in 1996.

The Illegal Immigration Reform and Immigrant Responsibility Act of 1996 (IIRAIRA) forbade local or state governments to place restrictions on the reporting of a person's immigration status to federal authorities, but it did not impose any affirmative duty to do so either.[24] As a result, the Major Cities Chiefs Association adopted a policy where member cities agree to work with federal authorities in apprehending illegal migrants suspected of committing a major crime, but not to help apprehend persons who are only suspected of being here illegally.[25]

Police chiefs and sheriffs in sixty-three U.S. cities and seven cities in Canada have expressed a lack of interest in cooperating with "catch and release" policies.[26] One reason for this is that undocumented people who have witnessed a crime or been the victim of a crime may not come forward for fear of removal proceedings.[27] Most police departments would rather solve a crime and get a perpetrator off the street than remove an undocumented person who might return anyway.

Conservative commentators accuse these cities of being "sanctuary cities," although they are not.[28] True "sanctuary cities" restrict the police from interfering in immigration matters. The term "sanctuary city" originated with the sanctuary movement for political prisoners from El Salvador and other Central America countries in the 1980s. In 1989, San Francisco became the most visible sanctuary city that actually was one.[29]

The Department of Homeland Security relies on the FBI's fingerprint data base in its Secure Communities Initiatives. The program claims to be primarily apprehending "criminal aliens" for deportation. A criminal alien is generally understood to be an undocumented person who has a criminal record in his native country or who has committed a serious crime here. However, as of March 2011, nearly thirty percent of the deportations under this program have been people with no criminal records. A patchwork of laws varying from state to state also presents problems in terms of the Constitution's "full faith and credit" clause.

Federal immigration authorities are spread too thin to accept custody of migrants detained for traffic violations or other minor offenses. IIRAIRA did lay the groundwork for a growing number of cities to cooperate with the Department of Homeland Security (DHS) through the 287(g) program. DHS claims this "law enforcement partnership" assists the federal government with its "broad responsibilities for a number of homeland security priorities." DHS wants to concentrate all its manpower on the border, and leave policing of the interior to state and local agencies.

Under the 287(g) program, local law enforcement officers who are trained and certified by the Department of Homeland Security can perform substantial immigration enforcement functions if, during the course of their normal duties, they encounter a foreign-born criminal or immigration violator *who poses a threat to national security or public safety* (italics are mine). A certified officer may question and detain an individual for potential removal from the United States.[30] The authority to conduct an immigration check extends only to the jail where the detainee must be charged and booked on a felony before any immigration check.

Some detainees complain of pretextual arrests which automatically lead to felony bookings. Civil rights groups feel that the immigration check should be made post conviction, not post arrest, but this practice is unlikely to change soon. These groups also say that the 287(g) program has no provision for meaningful oversight and they fear that the program has led to racial profiling. They also fear that the intimidation factor will take its toll on legal migrants in their communities.

Pseudo Crime

Some crime reporting comes with an agenda. One internet site stated that ninety-five percent of all outstanding homicide warrants in Los Angeles were for undocumented Hispanics.[31] That did not mean that Hispanics committed ninety-five percent of all homicides, or that ninety-five percent of all warrants issued were for Hispanics. It also does not mean that a jury would find all of those men guilty if they were served with warrants and brought to trial. The report only addressed individuals whom process servers could not find. Nonetheless, spin by some commentators on the right indicated that undocumented migrants committed ninety-five percent of all violent crime in Los Angeles.

Some crime reporting falls into the category of urban legend. Following the "Day without Immigrants" on May 1, 2006, the Los Angeles Police Department allegedly reported that violent crime was down forty-eight percent, the Los Angeles County Sheriff's Office allegedly reported that murders were down twenty-eight percent, and the California Highway Patrol allegedly reported that auto theft was down eighty-two percent. CNBC's "Wall Street Journal Report" allegedly reported that shoplifting nationwide was down 67.8 percent. These sources all denied making the reports, but large segments of the American public believed them anyway.[32]

In a 2006 paper entitled "The Dark Side of Illegal Immigration: Nearly One Million Sex Crimes Committed by Illegal Immigrants in the United States," Dr. Deborah Schurman-Kauflin, a psychologist, claimed that 240,000 Mexican sex offenders live in the United States, each has an average of four victims, and one hundred more enter the country every day. Dr. Schurman-Kauflin estimated that Mexicans had molested 960,000 Americans during the course of her study.[33] She reached her conclusions by doing grade school math on a 2003 General Accounting Office document which showed that two percent of all Hispanics *who were already incarcerated* (federal, state, or local) had been charged with a sex crime as a primary or a secondary charge. She then applied two percent to the estimated undocumented Hispanic population of twelve million and released her findings.

Raoul Lowery Contreras observed, "The fanatic Mexican and Hispanic haters generally do not have facts to back them up, no statistics that are worthy; they just make up their own facts, or take isolated instances and crank up the volume about Hispanic crime waves."[34]

Removal

The federal budget only provides enough money to deport about 400,000 people each year. Exclusion (keeping someone out) and deportation (removing a person who is already here) are now both called "removal. Both immigration judges and criminal judges can order removal. Health grounds for removal are limited, but tuberculosis is resuming exclusionary importance. Nearly one-third of all current tuberculosis cases in the United States are concentrated in California, Arizona, New Mexico, and Texas.[35] Gay applicants are no longer excluded, but AIDS patients are. A felony conviction can cause an application for admission to be rejected, as can a charge of moral turpitude, although foreign criminal records are often impossible to obtain or verify, and the definition of moral turpitude is highly subjective. Communists may now enter the country providing they don't advocate the violent overthrow of the U.S. government. Drug addicts may not enter the country.

An order of removal does not always result in removal. Many countries don't want their errant citizens back after they have committed a crime in another country and they refuse to issue travel documents for them. Cambodia, China, Cuba, Egypt, France, Gabon, Guyana, India, Laos, St. Vincent, Turkey, Vietnam, and the various former Soviet Republics are the worst offenders.[36]

Ironically, criminal aliens who do not want to be repatriated can make themselves ineligible for repatriation simply by refusing to cooperate with the U.S. government. If an alien has not served his full sentence, he must remain here until he has done so. If he has served his full sentence, and his native country refuses to take him back, the U.S. government has little alternative but to parole him into this country, barring acceptance by a third party country.

Notes

1 Paraphrased from The Sentencing Project, August 2003, citing J. Hagan and A. Palloni, "Sociological Criminology and the Mythology of Hispanic Immigrants and Crime," *Social Problems* 46 (1999): 617-32.

2 Steve Sailer, "Imprisonment Rates Vary Wildly by Race," *United Press International*, 14 Jun 2001, 6 Mar 2007 <http://www.isteve.com/CrimeImprisonment_Rates_by_Race htm>.

3 Patrick J. Buchanan, *State of Emergency* (New York: Holtzbrinck-St. Martin's Press, 2006), 25. Buchanan quotes the Federation for American Immigration Reform [FAIR].

4 United States, U.S. Department of Justice, Bureau of Justice Statistics, Office of Justice Programs, *Prison and Jail Inmates at Midyear 2005* by Paige M. Harrison and Allen J. Beck (Washington: GPO, 2006) 5.

5 Jennifer Steinhauer, "Immigration Law in Arizona Reveals G.O.P. Divisions," *The New York Times*, 22 May 2010 <http://www.nytimes.com/2010/05/21/us/politics/22immig.html>. (The article quotes the National Conference of State Legislators.)

6 Christopher Dickey, "Urban Legends," *Newsweek* 28 Nov 2007 <http://www.newsweek.com/id/72735/output>.

7 Ruben G. Rumbaut and Walter A. Ewing, "The Myth of Immigrant Criminality and the Paradox of Assimilation: Incarceration Rates among Native and Foreign-Born Men," Special Report (Immigration Policy Center, a division of the American Immigration Law Foundation, Spring 2007), 1.

8 Rumbaut, 14.

9 Rumbaut, 6. U.S. born Hispanics without a high school diploma are 11 times more likely to be incarcerated than foreign-born Hispanics without a high school diploma.

10 Ibid.

11 Rumbaut, *Myth of Immigrant*, 14.

12 Rumbaut, *Myth of Immigrant*, 14.

13 Rumbaut, *Myth of Immigrant*, 6.

14 United States. U.S. Department of Justice, Bureau of Prison Statistics, Office of Justice Programs, *Prisoners in 2007* by Heather C. West and William J. Sabol. (Washington: GPO, 2008) 6. Prisoners held in temporary facilities, such as drunk tanks or other facilities that do not hold persons after they are formally charged in court are not included. Also not included are prisoners held in other facilities mentioned at the beginning of the chapter.

15 *Prisoners in 2007*.

16 *Prisoners in 2007*.

17 *Prisoners in 2007*, 4.

18 *Prisoners in 2007*, 3.

19 United States. U.S. Department of Justice, Federal Justice Statistics Resource Center (a project of the Bureau of Justice Statistics), Fiscal Year 2007 *Prisoners in Federal Prison at Yearend*. This program allows the user to extract information from the Bureau of Prisons online Sentry System, standardized by the FJSRC. It allows the user to manipulate variables such as race, citizenship, ethnicity, and type of crime, 6 Jul 2009 <http://fjsrc.urban.org>.

20 *Prisoners in Federal Prison*.

21 "Facts about the Death Penalty," Death Penalty Information Center, 19 Jun 2007 <http://www.deathpenaltyinfo.org>.

22 United States. U.S. Department of Justice, Office of Justice Programs, *Capital Punishment by the Middle of the Next Century* Thomas P. Bonczar and Tracy L. Snell (Washington: GPO, 2004), 1, 9, 11.

23 "Foreign Nationals and the Death Penalty in the United States," *Death Penalty Information Center*. Based on research by Mark Warren, Human Rights Research, 5 Jun 2009, 7 Jun 2009 <www.deathpenaltyinfo.org>.

24 United States. House Judiciary Committee, New York City's Sanctuary Policy and the Effect of Such Policies (Washington: GPO, 2003).<http://

commdocs.house.gov/committees/judiciary/hju85287.000hju >.

25 Judy Keen, "Big Cities Reluctant to Target Illegals," *USA Today*, 20 Jun 2006: 1A.

26 Keen, "Big Cities."

27 *Sanctuary Policy*, 14.

28 Contrary to popular belief, there is no legal right to sanctuary in a church.

29 Jim Christie, "San Francisco to Give Illegal Aliens ID Cards," *Reuters*, 20 Nov 2007: 1.

30 United States. U.S. Immigration and Customs Enforcement, Department of Homeland Security, *Delegation of Immigration Authority, Section 287(g) Immigration and Nationality Act* (Washington: GPO, 2007), 1, 2.

31 Heather MacDonald, "The Illegal Alien Crime Wave," *City Journal* (2004), <http://www.cityjournal.org (21 Dec 2007)>.

32 "Talking Shop Lifting," *Urban Legends Reference*, 13 May 06, 30 May 2006 <http://snopes.com/politics/immigration/shoplift.asp>.

33 "Study: 1 Million Sex Crimes by Illegals: Researcher Estimates More Than 100 Offenders Crossing Border Daily," *WorldNetDaily*, 7 Oct 2007 <http://www.worldnetdaily.com/news/article/5044>.

34 Raoul Lowery Contreas, "A Hispanic Crime Wave That Isn't," *Latino Political Wires*, 6 Oct 2002, 20 Oct 2007 <http://www.voznuestra.com/PoliticalWires>.

35 Nancy Gibbs, "A Whole New World," *Time*, 11 Jun 2001: 42.

36 Ames Holbrook, *The Deporter: One Agent's Struggle against the United States Government's Refusal to Expel Criminal Aliens* (New York, NY: Sentinel-Penguin, 2007), 11. The federal budget only provides enough money to deport about 400,000 people each year.

Photo Credit: Vincent Blaine

Chapter Six

NATIONAL SECURITY

The U.S. Immigration and Customs Enforcement Service (ICE)

U.S. BORDER Patrol agents are today's "revenuers." When the United States wanted to control intoxicating liquors, they did it with a repressive law—the Eighteenth Amendment to the Constitution. Thirteen years later, the Twenty-first Amendment recognized reality and repealed the Eighteenth Amendment. The reality of a workable U.S.-Mexican border solution has yet to be recognized by the U.S. government.

In some ways, the powers of the U.S. Immigration and Customs Enforcement Service (ICE), under the Department of Homeland Security, exceed those of the FBI and the CIA. Without a warrant, ICE agents can board any boat, plane, train, or ship, or enter any private land or dwelling within twenty-five miles of a border. Probable cause is not required; reasonable suspicion will do. Miranda warnings are not required, although they may be used if criminal prosecution, such as a drug charge, is anticipated.

Despite what one hears from political candidates wanting to make unauthorized border crossing a felony, entering without inspection (EWI) appears to have been a felony since 1929 – it's a matter of interpretation.[1] Most other immigration offenses—up to and including removal—are civil offenses, and do not give the offender a criminal record.

The Sixth Amendment's right to an attorney does not apply in immigration law. Federal rules of evidence do not apply, hearsay evidence is admissible, good evidence trumps bad procedure, evidence cannot be suppressed, new charges can be added in the middle of a proceeding, and hearings can be closed or held *in abstentia*. However, non English-speaking detainees *are* entitled to a translator.

During times of heightened public concern about immigration, especially in communities that both rely on and resent illegal workers, ICE raids of apartment complexes, packinghouses, and bus stations command a great deal of press coverage. Demands for better control at the border and calls for all immigration offenses to be criminalized are common. However, they present constitutional problems, and invite well-funded challenges from business and industry to insure that they will go nowhere.

Border Security

At the end of the Cold War, the America military needed a new mission and took on the drug war so they would have something to do. The War on Drugs ™ officially began on December 21 1970, when Richard Nixon "deputized" Elvis Presley in the Oval Office.[2] Since September 11, 2001, U.S. citizens have demanded that the federal government regain control of its borders. The word "regain" suggests that the borders have ever been under control, which has never been the case.

Security decisions require understanding the difference between hypothetical risks and actual risks. Former U.S. Surgeon General C. Everett Koop differentiated between the two when he wrote about the cyclamate scare based on experimentation with rats that took his favorite soft drink off the market. "I would have had to drink four bathtubs full of Fresca every day for about eight years to have an equivalent dosage," he wrote.[3] The threat of international terrorism along the Mexican-American border is today's cyclamate.

Border security revolves around three issues: illegal migration, drug trafficking, and the threat of terrorism. Two of these issues, illegal migration and drug trafficking, are based on the laws of supply and demand—the United States wants cheap labor and its citizens are the world's most lucrative market for illicit drugs. For a time after 9-11, the U.S. was legitimately occupied with the serious possibility of terrorism on all fronts. With the passage of time, however, the government should have been able to sort out which things are actual risks and which ones are not, but they claim they have not been able to so.

Further, U.S. border security is only concerned with things that enter the border. It ignores a healthy trade in things that leave the border, such as untaxed cigarettes, pharmaceuticals, laundered money, firearms, alcohol, computer chips, stolen cars, stolen babies, child prostitutes, fissionable material, pornography, antiquities, exotic animals, precious metals, gemstones, and human organs.[28]

Drugs

There are over four million cocaine users in the United States. This accounts for more than one third of the world's consumption of the white powder. The hunger for drugs in the United States is always blamed on factors outside of the country. The United States looks for supply-side solutions to eliminate the cultivation and processing of drugs before they reach U.S. soil. Carlos Fuentes wrote, "It is easier. . .to militarize Bolivia than to militarize the Bronx."[4]

In terms of cocaine, a specialization exists between Peruvians, the primary growers of coca; Colombians, the primary processors; and Mexicans, the primary transporters. Other South American countries, notably Bolivia and Brazil, are also involved. This specialization is the result of U.S. anti-drug policy in the southeastern coastal areas of United States and American control of Pacific and Gulf sea lanes, which has forced Colombians to rely on Mexicans to move drugs from South America across the Mexican-American border into the United States.[5]

A middle assumption of 330 metric tons of cocaine entering the United States each year would require three Boeing 707s to transport it.[6] On one occasion, smugglers actually flew a Boeing 727 from northern Mexico into the United States. On another occasion, a French-made Caravelle was used. Each flight carried six tons of cocaine.[7] Colombian drug cartels have also been using small semi-submersibles, or narcosubs, since the 1990s.[8]

But foreign drug cartels cannot carry out their illegal enterprise alone. Trafficking on this scale requires the cooperation of stateside financiers, money launderers, and wealthy Americans who own helicopters, private jets, cargo planes, hangers, warehouses, wharfs, small speedboats, and large ships. Nor could this volume of illegal drugs enter this country without the help of corrupt U.S. air traffic controllers, prosecutors, judges, baggage handlers, politicians, U.S. customs agents, border patrol officers, National Guardsmen, and local law enforcement personnel. In 2007, MSNBC reported that the U.S. government had investigated 288 employees of U.S. Customs and Border Enforcement since 2004.[9]

Historically, the main opponents of border security have been politicians from southwestern states who are influenced by campaign contributions from agribusiness and other commercial concerns in their districts.[10] Undocumented workers do not make campaign contributions.

The drug problem in the United States is much greater in scale than peasants crossing the border with a small amount of marijuana hidden under a bandana. However, both drug smugglers and U.S. customs agents have their uses for small drug shipments. Smugglers use them to distract customs inspectors, and customs inspectors use them to inflate their interdiction statistics, even though they are not related to the actual amount of drugs that get through.[11]

In 1998, Pat Buchanan wrote, "We should cancel that provision of NAFTA which permits Mexican trucks on America's highways. . .expand the border patrol. . .lengthen the fence already built at San Diego. . .[bring] home troops from abroad [and move them to] the southern border."[12] Buchanan did not address the problem of demand for drugs in the U.S.

Terrorists

The U.S.- Mexico border is 1,952 miles long. Americans are told that this border is the most vulnerable to terrorist attack. If Al Qaeda operatives tried to enter the United States from Mexico, they would have to get past vicious *narcotraficantes*, corrupt units of the Mexican military or state police, an inhospitable desert crawling with rattlesnakes, pit vipers, and tarantulas, and a ground temperature that can reach 160 degrees Fahrenheit.

In reality, terrorists do not need to sneak through the southern border. They can easily enter the United States legally on student visas, or as businessmen or tourists, just as the 9-11 terrorists did. People of all ethnic or racial backgrounds are able to blend in because of the diversity of the U.S. population.

On the other hand, Roberto Suro pointed out, "If Wal-Mart can account for its inventory, the United States certainly can track its visitors."[27] During the "mad cow" scare of 2002, U.S. Department of Agriculture inspectors were able to track truckloads of Canadian cows to the United States, know where they slept, what they ate, and where their calves were. The U.S. government should be able to track its visitors as well as it can track cows.

The government's use of an artificial threat of terrorism does have precedent. The U.S. Postal Service long had difficulties with homeless people at many of their urban facilities. Immediately after 9-11, the government closed many facilities to box holders who had paid for twenty-four-hour access. In the name of fighting terrorism, these postal patrons had their access cut in half, with no notice and no refund. If the federal government cannot control homeless people in post office lobbies, they are not going to have much luck with terrorists.

The foregoing also misses the threat of homegrown terrorists. Once easily identified geographically and ideologically, their threat is now ubiquitous. For example, there are militias and survivalists, Christian Identity, the Aryan Brotherhood, the Klan, the Posse Comitatus, the Patriot Movement, and Sovereign Citizens.

Prior to 9-11, the most heinous terrorist event in the United States was the bombing of the Murrah Federal Building in Oklahoma City. Sealing the southern border would not have prevented the loss of 167 lives there. A sealed border would not have thwarted the massacre in Littleton, Colorado or Seung-Hui Cho's killing spree at Virginia Tech. It would not have prevented the unibomber, Ruby Ridge, the D.C. snipers, the deaths in Waco, or the shootings at the Olympic Games in Atlanta. Sealing the southern border would not have deterred the underpants bomber, the rampage of Major Nadal Hasan at Fort Hood, Texas, or the murders in Tucson. The term, "border security" makes people feel good when they hear it, but it is just a smokescreen to camouflage America's failed drug and immigration policies. "Border security" has little to do with national security.

Distinguishing between terrorism, drugs, and migrants is not hard—terrorists and drugs do harm; migrants harvest crops and do the ironing. Michael Chertoff, former head of the Department of Homeland Security, said, "Every time a border patrol officer is transporting a load of future housekeepers and landscapers to some place to be returned, he's not looking for drug dealers ..."[29] Mr. Chertoff made no mention of terrorists. The American economy suffers when a necessary and industrious workforce is used as a scapegoat for the nation's real problems.

The Virtual Wall

> In his poem *Mending Wall*, Robert Frost is frequently misquoted as saying, "good fences make good neighbors." Actually, it was the poet's neighbor who spoke those words. What Frost said was, "Before I build a wall I'd ask to know what I was walling in or walling out, and to whom I was like to give offense. Something there is that doesn't love a wall, that wants it down."[13]

Unlike most counties, the United States is fortunate in that it only shares its borders with two countries. Contrary to popular perception, the northern border with Canada poses as much of a terrorism threat as the southern border with Mexico does, possibly more. The 5,525-mile long American-Canadian border is the longest undefended border in the world.[14] The "millennium bomber" was caught there.[15] National parks that adjoin the Canadian border have long reported drug trafficking there, but no barrier along that border has ever been suggested.[16] The Canadian border or the 12,479 miles of U.S. shoreline are seldom mentioned in debates about border security because the federal government is not as concerned with international terrorism or drug trafficking as it is with the public's clamor over illegal migration from the south.

The government's border plan was to construct a concrete and steel barrier from the Pacific Ocean to the Gulf of Mexico, and electrify as much of it as possible. Representative Silvestre Reyes (D-TX) called the project "expensive and a waste of taxpayer's money."[17] Reyes is a former El Paso Sector Chief for the U.S. Border Patrol. The late Molly Ivins suggested that the government could give a no bid contract to Halliburton, and let them build the wall with undocumented labor.[18]

Any kind of barricade would cost billions of dollars, deter nothing, and encourage the smuggling industry. The section of the wall south of San Diego only shifted illegal migration to Arizona; it did not stop it. Migrants will find some way around, under, or over anything the government builds. The Barry Goldwater bombing range and Fort Huachuca, an Army Intelligence Center, both in Arizona, do not deter migrants.

Still, Boeing was awarded a three-year, $69 million dollar contract for "Project 28," the first twenty-eight miles of a barrier in Texas (similar to the one in California) augmented by sensors, cameras, and other untested electronic gadgetry. These devices did not deliver as promised.[19]

Many border residents felt that money should have been funneled into hiring and training more border patrol officers. President Bush announced plans to boost the number of officers by 5,500, from 12,500 to 18,000 before leaving office. At the beginning of 2011, the actual result of that initiative was a force of 20,500 officers.

From an environmental point of view, the project required moving billions of tons of earth in order to install twelve to sixteen foot high sections of single or double carbon steel fencing and wire mesh. Environmentalists say the construction upset the area's ecological balance, and disrupted migratory habits of wildlife. Ranchers on both sides of the Rio Grande *(Rio Bravo)* worried about their continued access to water.

By 2008, the rush to finish the wall overrode these and all other interests. The Secretary of Homeland Security was given the authority to void any and all other laws in order to get the wall built.[20]

In 2006, President Bush announced plans for an additional 670 miles of wall construction, approximately the distance from Atlanta to Chicago, and President Obama indicated his intent to follow through on the project. The Department of Homeland Security estimated that the total cost could be as high as $30 billion dollars, but one of the hidden costs was maintenance.[20] A report by the Congressional Research Service in 2006 predicted that costs for maintenance alone could reach $70 million dollars over the next twenty-five years.[21] Three years later, estimates had jumped to $600 million dollars![22]

Older sections of the wall in California had deteriorated and were broken through regularly.[23] Pieces of the wall were carted off and sold for scrap. The estimates for the wall did not include replacement of these sections. Estimates also did not include land acquisition, labor, sensors, lighting, surveillance cameras, equipment rental, the cost for the National Guard, or money to fight potential lawsuits.[24] (The Guard is able to provide some assistance to the border patrol, but they can not make arrests.)

One section of the "virtual wall" in Arizona only yielded fifty-three miles at an average cost of $15 million a mile. The "virtual wall" was a part of a larger Homeland Security project called SBInet which was plagued with technical glitches from the beginning. The entire 1,952 miles of the Mexican-American border was supposed to be completed by 2011. Not counting the original section in California, only eighty-one miles were actually completed when Homeland Security Secretary Janet Napolitano cancelled the project completely in 2011.[25] Napolitano then used $50 million left over from SBInet to invest in drones, thermal imaging devices and other surveillance equipment previously proven unreliable in SBInet.[26]

Napolitano's actions did not sit well with Arizona residents. A state government website allows citizens to donate to a fund so that Arizona can finish the barrier by itself. The state hopes to raise $50 million dollars through tax deductible donations.

Documentation for Migrants

"For years there has been an explicit understanding among businesses that need workers, migrants who are willing to work, communities that benefit from such commerce, and governments that rarely intervene."[30] Recently, there has been a renewed demand that migrant workers have better identification. More recently yet, there has also been a demand for U.S. citizens to have better identification.

Secretary Chertoff said that there used to be over eight thousand different types of identification acceptable for entry into the United States. He said it was unreasonable to expect border inspectors to be able to detect forgeries when dealing with such a large range of documents. That number was winnowed down to about two dozen in 2008.

When dealing with the question of a migrant's documentation, there are a few things to remember. An American citizen may *ask* for a voluntary show of documents, but they should always have some overriding purpose for doing so. Curiosity or suspicion are not acceptable reasons. (Many Americans do not routinely carry anything on their person that proves their U.S. citizenship.)

Only an immigration official, a commissioned law enforcement officer, or an employer can *demand* to see a migrant's documentation. In law enforcement, this demand can only be made after a suspect has been booked and charged with a felony (see Chapter Five). Employers cannot demand to see documents until after they have actually offered a job to a prospective employee.

There is another reason for caution besides the lack of legal authority; "green cards" have not been green since 1959. If a person does not know what a "green card" looks like, why would they ask to see one?

There is an oft-repeated story from the 1970s about a department store chain that sold wallets with realistic looking Social Security cards inside which resulted in 33,000 undocumented workers trying to file on the same Social Security number.[31] False documents abound, and many are quite good, or good enough—since border inspectors often spend less than one minute per inspection. A virtually undetectable set of documents cost between $400.00 and $1,000.00 in 2009. These might include a driving permit, marriage license, baptismal certificate, school records, and a Social Security card.

The *"Matricula Consular"* is an official Mexican ID. Some other Latin American countries have similar documents. The laminated Matricula is tamper proof, unlike the unlaminated American Social Security card. The main problem with a *Matricula* is that the Mexican government requires no proof that the documents used to obtain it are legitimate. Even though the *Matricula* is an official Mexican government document, migrants using one in the United States are still subject to arrest and removal if they are here illegally.

E-Verify for Employers

E-Verify (formerly called Basic Pilot) is a free program promoted by the Department of Homeland Security in conjunction with the Social Security Administration. It is seriously flawed unless and accept when it is linked to a fingerprint data base or a biometric identity system. The government does not claim it to be otherwise. The General Accounting Office and the Social Security Administration have complained about the program's unacceptably high error rates. In 2007, only eleven percent of the nation's private employers used the system because it was so unreliable.[32] A Department of Homeland Security study in 2009 found that Legal Permanent Residents and naturalized citizens were twenty times more likely to be erroneously singled out than native-born U.S. citizens.[33]

Federal contractors were not required to use E-Verify until 2010 and only for new hires after that. Three states require it; several other states are seeking to mandate it. Tribal governments are exempt. Contracts for less than $100,000.00 or 120 days are also exempt.[34] Most private contractors are not required to use the program but if they do they cannot be held liable for any mistakes, although their employees can be arrested.

"Real ID" for United States Citizens

The "Real ID" Act is a piece of federal legislation aimed at American citizens, which was scheduled to go into effect on May 11th, 2008, but the Department of Homeland Security has given the states a third extension to January 15th, 2013. The ID card was originally envisioned to have a bar code and encryption so that taverns and other types of businesses would not be able to scan it.[35] Department of Motor Vehicle employees in every state would be subject to background checks to protect against insider fraud, and they would have to verify the documents used to procure the new licenses. The Act also aimed at creating a linkage between all the states' databases so it would be difficult for *indocumentados* to get a "Real ID" driver's license, or for anyone to have more than one.[36]

Congress watered the bill down because they feared that Real ID would become a real nightmare. By the time of passage, the legislation only targeted a few states that did not already include certain minimum information on their licenses. In order to force compliance, the federal government said that residents of states which contest the legislation will not be able to board airplanes, enter federal buildings, or visit national parks with their old driver's licenses, although they will be able to do so with other documents such as a passport.[37] Maryland is considering a two-tiered approach where residents who actually need a "Real ID" could pay extra for it.

The Wall Street Journal editorialized, "Real ID was always more about harassing Mexican illegals than stopping Islamic terrorists."[38] The ACLU is opposed to "Real ID" and more than half of the state legislatures have proposed or passed legislation indicating that they will not comply with Congress. Some estimates for implementation run as high as $11 billion dollars nationwide. So far, only a handful of states have reached an agreement with the Department of Homeland Security for secure licenses.

A bold step like "Real ID" is sure to fail when the United States has not succeeded even when it has tried identification reform in gradual steps. A Transport Workers Identification Card has been stalled for years, and a Seaport Workers Identification Card, scheduled for use in 2007, suffered the same fate.[39]

It is also unlikely that the United States can take the lead with other nations when it has unresolved identification problems of its own. Latin American nations do not place a high priority on the identification issue and will not do so until the U.S. gives them either positive or negative incentives for doing so.

Notes

1 Manuel G. Gonzales, *Mexicanos* (Bloomington: Indiana UP, 2000), 147.

2 Egil "Bud" Krogh, *The Day Elvis Met Nixon* (Bellevue: Pejama Press, 1994).

3 C. Everett Koop, "Good Words About Pesticides," My Thoughts, *Progressive Farmer* 107.1 (1992): 16.

4 Carlos Fuentes, *A New Time for Mexico* (Berkeley: California UP, 1997), 174.

5 Peter Andreas, "Creating the Clandestine Side of the Border Economy," *Border Games: Policing the U.S.-Mexico Divide* (Ithaca: Cornell UP, 2000), 44.

6 *Substance Abuse: A Comprehensive Textbook*, 3rd ed. Eds. Joyce A. Lowinson, Pedro Ruiz, Robert B. Millman, and John G. Langrod, (Baltimore: Williams and Wilkins, 1997).

7 David C. Jordan, *Drug Politics: Dirty Money and Democracies* (Norman: Oklahoma UP, 1999), 151.

8 William Booth and Juan Ferero, "Plying the Pacific, Subs Surface as Key Tool of Drug Cartels," *The Washington Post Foreign Service*, 6 Jun 2009, 7 Jun 2009 <http://www.washingtonpost.com/wp-dyn>.

9 Arian Campo-Flores and Monica Campbell, "Iraq War Hero Charged with Human Smuggling," *Newsweek*, 16 Jul 2007 <http://www.msnbc.com/id/19651930>.

10 Gonzalez, *Mexicanos*, 176.

11 Peter Andreas, "The Escalation of Immigration Control," *Border Games: Policing the United States-Mexico Divide* (Ithaca: Cornell University Press, 2000), 79, 83.

12 Patrick J. Buchanan, *The Great Betrayal: How American Sovereignty and Social Justice Are Being Sacrificed to the Gods of the Global Economy* (New York: Little Brown, 1998), 318.

13 Robert Frost, "Mending Wall," *The Top 500 Poems, A Columbia Anthology*, Ed. William Harmon (New York: Columbia UP, 1992), 897, 898.

14 Paul R. Pillar, *Terrorism and United States Foreign Policy* (Washington: Brookings Institute Press, 2001), 58.

15 Ted Robbins, "Q&A: Building a Barrier along the Border with Mexico," *National Public Radio*, 27 May 2007 <http://www.NPR.org/storyID5326083>.

16 Judd Slivka, "It's the Wild West Every Night Along Border," (reprinted from *The Arizona Republic*) *USA Today*, 5 Nov 2003: 20 A.

17 Johnson, "In the Southwest," 2A.

18 Molly Ivins, "One More Round of Blame the Immigrant," *Fort Worth Star Telegram*, 9 Jul 2006: 6E.

19 Spencer S. Hsu, "In Virtual Fence, Continuity with Border Effort by Bush," *The Washington Post*, 9 Jun 2009 <http://www.washingtonpost.com/wp/dyn>.

20 Adam Liptak, Sidebar, "Border Fence Project Can Void Any Law, but Challenges Arise," New York Times, 8 Mar 2008: A1.

20 Kevin Johnson, "In the Southwest, Fixing the Fence Never Ends: Damage to Old Walls Puts Focus on Repair Costs in 700 mile Plan," *USA Today*, 16 Sep 2007: 1 A, 2A.

21 J. Lynn Lunsford and Robert Block, "Can a 'Virtual Fence' Help Seal United States Border?" *Wall Street Journal*, 5 Jun 2007: A 2.

22 Robbins, "Building a Barrier."

23 Johnson, "In the Southwest," 2A.

24 United States. General Accounting Office, *Secure Border Initiative Fence Construction Cost*, 29 Jan 2009, 10 Aug 2009 <http://www.gao.gov/new.items/d09244r.pdf>. There were at least five different types of fencing that were used along the border with as many cost variables. Examples are labor costs for National Guard installed fence compared to the costs for private contractors, the type of fence, terrain, and the cost of material in different years. Some work cost as little as $200,000.00 per mile while one particular mile cost $15.1 million dollars. At a minimum, the average cost is 3.5 million dollars per mile, probably much more.

25 "Obama Administration Ends High-Tech Border Fence," the Associated Press, *National Public Radio*, 14 January 2010:1 <http://www.NPR.org/123940996/obama-administration-ends high-tech-border-fence>.

26 "Homeland Security Chief Cancels Costly Border Fence," Wire Staff, CNN, 14 Jan 2011 <http://www.cnn.com/2011/US/01/14/border.virtual.fence/index.html?eref=mrss-igoogle-cnn>.

27 Roberto Suro, *Strangers Among Us: Latino Lives in a Changing America* (New York: Vintage-Random House, 1999), 274.

28 Andreas, "The Political Economy of Global Smuggling," *Border Games*, 16.

29 Michael Chertoff during his first official visit to Mexico, "Verbatim," *Time*, 5 Mar 2007: 9. During his first official visit to Mexico, the former Homeland Security Secretary spoke on the need to create a guest-worker program so that U.S. law enforcement can focus on terrorists and other criminals.

30 Susan Berfield, "Illegals and Business: A Glimpse of the Future?" *Business Week*, 3 Jan 2008 <http://www.businessweek.com/magazine/content/08>.

31 Ted Conover, *Coyotes: A Journey through the Secret World of America's Illegal Aliens* (New York: Vintage-Random House, 1987), 207.

32 June Kronholz and Sarah Lueck, "Senate Immigration Measure to Raise Liability for Employers," Politics and Economics, *Wall Street Journal*, 22 May 2007: A6.

33 Nina Totenberg, Supreme Court Tests Ariz. Law Targeting Employers who Hire Illegal Immigrants, *National Public Radio*, 12 December 2008 <http://www.NPR.org/2010/12/08/131884244/high-court-tests-ariz-law-targeting-emplo...htm>.

34 "Most Federal Contractors Must E-Verify under New Rule," *Perkins Coie News/Publications*, 8 Jan 2009 <http://perkinscoie.com/news/pubs>.

35 Declan McCullagh, "Homeland Security Offers Details on Real ID," 1 Mar 2007 <http://c/net/news.com.Homeland+Security>.

36 United States. Department of Homeland Security, *"Real ID" Preserving Our Freedoms* <http://popularsearches.DHS.index.gov/html>.

37 McCullagh, "Homeland Security."

38 "Real ID Revolt," Review and Outlook, *Wall Street Journal*, 8 May 2007: A18.

39 Pam Fessler, "Delays Plague Homeland Security ID Project," The Nation, *National Public Radio*, 30 Jun 2007 <http://www.NPR.org>.

PRESS ONE FOR ENGLISH

Photo Credit: Vincent Blaine

Chapter Seven

ASSIMILATION

On May 1, 2006, "A Day without Immigrants," many Americans were offended by crowds of Hispanics singing "The Star Spangled Banner" ("*la bandera de las estrellas*") in Spanish. One thing is certain: Americans have some raw nerves on the issue.

However, what the public did not know was that the original Spanish language translation was commissioned by the United States Bureau of Education in 1919, and the U.S. government is now the copyright holder of five Spanish language versions of the national anthem.[1]

These translations are to help newly arrived Spanish-speaking individuals express respect for the flag before or while they learn English.

The other newsmaker of that day was over "unpatriotic" celebrants waving the Mexican flag. Irish Americans are apparently exempt from similar complaints when they fly the Irish flag on Saint Patrick's Day.

Singing the "Star Spangled Banner" in Spanish and displaying flags of other countries are both covered by the First Amendment.

Assimilation

The three stages of a migrant's adjustment to a new environment are adaptation, acculturation, and assimilation. The terms are not interchangeable.

Adaptation is the simple adjustment to the everyday realities of the host environment, such as understanding the meaning of street signs. Some migrants won't progress much beyond this stage, but most will show some degree of acculturation in using the host language, eating local food, and venturing outside of the migrant community. Assimilation is completely adopting the attitudes and behaviors of the host community.

Migrants with children are more likely to assimilate than migrants without children. Marriage into the dominant culture or service in the armed forces represent a high level of assimilation. The rate of assimilation is also affected by geography: vast oceans separate European and Asian migrants from their homeland, language, families, friends, culture, and support mechanisms. For Mexicans, home is just a stone's throw away and this is a major factor in their assimilation, or lack of it.

The incidence of obesity, diabetes, and high blood pressure increases the longer migrants live in the United States, along with an increased risk for drug and alcohol addiction.[2] A rise in the incidence of mental illness may also be a marker for assimilation.[3]

Barrios and Borderlands

Many migrants—documented or not—begin their American experience in ethnic enclaves, called *barrios*, where they attempt to recreate their homeland. New migrants may receive financial assistance, help in finding a job, or moral support from friends or relatives who came before them. *Barrios* offer migrants the opportunity to make friends, shop, worship, and conduct business in their native language, so some migrants may perceive that there is little to be gained from learning English (see Appendices IV and V).

As the better-skilled or better educated migrants acculturate or assimilate and move out of the *barrio*, a less desirable population is left behind—often poorly educated in their own country, and undocumented in this country. *Barrios* create environments that are dysfunctional, and dysfunctional environments breed crime and other destructive behaviors. *Barrios* can be as destructive as poverty or drugs. It is generally from *barrio* residents that native-born Americans form their first opinions about migrants. Eliminating *barrios* and encouraging English language skills will speed up assimilation.

In Miami, Florida, Cubans have created what is probably the world's largest *barrio*. It is the only *barrio* in the United States that is both affluent and influential. The early Cuban migrants came to the United States because of their hatred of Fidel Castro. Many *Cubanos* claim to be *exiles*, not immigrants, although it is doubtful that many of them would ever return to Cuba.

Barrio landlords bear much of the blame for the problems of the *barrios*. The purpose of any business is to make a profit, and being a *barrio* landlord should not involve taking the place of law enforcement or social welfare agencies. However, it is axiomatic that increased neighborhood degradation will yield increased crime, and property owners have a responsibility to the larger community not to be active participants in behaviors that threaten the common good.

Native-born citizens seeking to rent must submit to a credit check, a criminal background check, and a prior rental history. This is often difficult with legal immigrants, and impossible with undocumented renters. Slumlords will rent to anyone, including undesirable elements of their own community. If slumlords screened all tenants uniformly and required solid identification, they would go a long way toward improving the *barrio* situation. Solid identification does not necessarily mean proof of legal status.

Even when slumlords go through the motions of executing a normal rental agreement, they may not have any idea who is living in their property after just a few months time. For example, a slumlord may rent an apartment to a married couple with acceptable (although possibly false) identification. Soon, one or two friends or relatives will move in, and the couple will move out. The secondary tenants will bring in a few of their friends, co-workers, or relatives. The slumlord's records may show the names of the two original tenants for years, while the couple repeats the cycle of acquiring housing for their countrymen over and over at new locations.

In the ghetto, public safety issues abound. There may be four or five automobiles where there should only be one or two, the drivers will almost certainly be unlicensed, their vehicles may not be tagged or insured, and parking will be at a premium. Municipal services may be strained, there will be more noise, an increase in abandoned vehicles, an increased risk of fire, heavier traffic, and the need for an increased police presence. These conditions will lead to conflict with residents in the adjoining neighborhoods, which can lead to "white flight."

Borderlands areas have many the same characteristics as a *barrio*, only borderlands are much larger. Some scholars describe a borderlands area as being ten to twenty-five miles on either side of a border.[4] Others see borderlands regionally, as much as several hundred miles on either side of a border. The Miami-Dade area, being a coastal interface between the United States and Cuba, is both a *barrio* and a borderlands area.

"No Interest" Mexican Credit

Undocumented Hispanics pay exorbitant prices for their automobiles. They have no choice. They probably don't know any better, either. If a car is advertised, "*Enganche $500*," it means that the dealer paid $500.00 for the car at an auction, and when the migrant pays $500.00 down, the dealer is actually paid in full. However, the migrant might pay $50.00 per week for the next two years, making the total price of the $500 car $5,300.00. A jalopy advertised for $1,000.00 down, $100.00 per week, will ultimately cost $10,100.00.

Dealers promote this as "interest free financing," and the migrant thinks he has *crédito*. Since 2004, many "Katrina cars" have shown up on car lots catering to migrants. It is not uncommon for a high mileage clunker to give out before the term of the note. If the migrant defaults on his payments, the dealer repossess the car, keeps everything that he was paid, and, if the car is running, sells it again, possibly more than once. The obligation for the total purchase price is still enforceable on the original purchaser. When Hispanics do this to other Hispanics, it's called "the American way."

Driving While Brown

Americans want homes built, roads maintained, crops harvested, shirts ironed, yards mowed, tables bussed and thousands of other jobs that are performed by migrants every day. Like everyone else, migrants have to get back and forth to work, but most Americans do not want them to drive. The thinking is that if migrants do not have a license, they will not drive. Instead, this creates more unlicensed drivers and more uninsured motorists.

Undocumented migrants can buy an automobile, but they cannot get a driver's license without proof of legal status, except in a handful of states that have decided that legal entry has nothing to do with experience, maturity, or competency behind the wheel. Where *indocumentados* are allowed to drive, the states recognize two basic public safety issues: (1) that the state has a right to know who the drivers are, and (2) that all motorists should be able to pass a driving test.

In New Mexico, undocumented workers have been driving legally since 2003. According to the *Wall Street Journal*, police in New Mexico state that their roads are safer since undocumented migrants have been able to obtain driver's licenses.[5] A Nevada Department of Motor Vehicles spokesman quoted in the same article said, "It's not our issue if you are in the country illegally [but] by law, you have to have insurance if you have a car."[6] In Utah, undocumented workers can qualify for a "driving privilege card," distinct from a driver's license.[7]

New York almost joined these states in 2008. An aide to then New York Governor Eliot Spitzer said, "The facts show that restricting an immigrant's access to a driver's license does nothing to improve security. All it does is drive immigrants into the shadows, creating a class of people with no public records."[8] Two weeks later, the Governor succumbed to public pressure and withdrew the plan. Hawaii, Maryland, Michigan, North Carolina, Oregon, Tennessee, and Washington have considered or rescinded similar programs in recent years.

In states where *indocumentados* cannot legally obtain a driver's license, it also usually means that they will not have a valid license plate on their car, or that their car may not be registered at all. However, for a monthly fee, called a *mordida* (little bite), dishonest car dealers will indefinitely renew a temporary tag for a person who purchased a vehicle from them, and sometimes, if the price is right, for people who purchased their cars elsewhere.

The lack of a driver's license and a valid license plate generally predicts a lack of insurance. One option is for a migrant to find a legal resident who will insure the vehicle for him—for a price. Legal residents can insure up to the number of vehicles that would require a dealer's license in their state, usually ten or twelve. The usual option for most migrants is not to have any automobile insurance.

Recently, the American free enterprise system stepped in to fill this void. Some insurers view undocumented migrants as a great, untapped market, and increasingly insurers are offering policies to them, with or without a driver's license.[9] Because an *indocumentados* driving record is not verifiable, premiums will be well above the market rate. Now that migrants can get automobile insurance, native-born citizens who previously complained about uninsured migrants are now complaining about "un-American" companies selling insurance to them.

Politics, Business and Religion

Politics are central to any discussion of migration. If asked which political party is most associated with migrants, the average person will answer "the Democrats." However, for the most part, it was Republican investors who owned stock in the steamship lines that brought immigrants to this country, or who owned the tenement houses where they originally lived, the railroads that took them west, or the factories and corporate farms where many of their descendants still toil today. It should also be remembered that the amnesty where nearly three million migrants were legalized in 1986, came during the administration of a Republican president, Ronald Reagan.[10]

Migration has always been a product of the capital required for business, and big business has historically been associated with Republicans. It is no different today. Democrats have long been tainted by their association with organized labor, which until recently was very anti-immigration. However, until 2000, Democrats generally received a majority of the Hispanic vote because of that party's identification with social issues that concerned them.

President George W. Bush consistently pursued a pro-immigration agenda even though it contradicted the mood of the public. In 2000, candidate Bush won the Hispanic vote in general, and a high percentage of the Cuban-American vote, although the latter had much to do with Al

Gore's waffling during the Elian Gonzalez affair (see Appendix I). But Elian was long gone by 2004, when President Bush doubled his percentage of the Hispanic vote. The president also picked up 78 percent of the evangelical vote in 2004.[11]

There has always been a connection between Hispanic religious expression and politics, although the focus has shifted. Most Latin Americans were brought up as Catholics, and at the beginning of the last century there were few Protestants in Latin America.[12] Mainline Protestant denominations did not send missionaries there, but Mormons, Jehovah's Witnesses, and various evangelical denominations aggressively proselytized the region, referring to their efforts as *la cosecha*, or "the harvest." By the 1980s, Latin Catholicism was being challenged by liberation theology, which played well to liberal members of the priesthood, most of whom were from Europe, but not to the indigenous masses.

For many worshippers, dynamic evangelical services with up-beat music and the promise of a rich life in Christ were better received than Catholic services extolling the Savior's poverty and suffering. Another difference between Catholics and evangelicals is that in the Catholic Church, the priest has absolute control, but in Protestant churches, the congregation does.

In Guatemala, "prosperity theology" is attracting the poorest citizens to the evangelical cause, and they already represent nearly twenty percent of the population.[13] In general, evangelicals are the fastest growing religious movement in North America, and they are the fastest growing form of religious expression within the Hispanic community as well. Hispanics who are native to the United States, and the millions of Mexicans and Central Americans who have migrated here since the 1990s, have embraced the message and promise of the evangelicals.

Evangelicals are a core constituency of the Republican Party, and the values of the Hispanic evangelicals are much closer to the "family values" of the Republican Party than to the values of the Democrats, who are fragmented over environmental, gender, and labor issues.

Today, there are more than fifty million Protestants in Latin America, and most of them are members of evangelical or charismatic churches.[14]

The region could be predominantly Protestant and evangelical by the end of the twenty-first century.[15] The tremendous growth of the evangelical Hispanic church has translated into membership and money, actively courted in the U.S. by both political parties. The fact that millions of the faithful are undocumented and cannot vote makes little difference: denominational capital equals political capital.

Both of George Bush's victories relied on Hispanics and evangelicals. These groups are twice as likely as Catholics to identify as Republican.[16] In 2000, Bush carried thirty-five percent of the Hispanic vote.[17] In 2004, exit polls showed forty-four percent of Hispanic voters said they voted Republican.[18] George Bush was poised to be remembered as the man who brought millions of Hispanics into the Republican fold, but the tables turned again. After the 2006 mid-term elections, the Republican's share of the Hispanic vote dropped to twenty-nine percent, presumably because Hispanic voters felt that the Republicans had not delivered on their promises.[19] In the 2008 elections, Hispanics voted heavily Democratic, and gave Barack Obama sixty-seven percent of their vote over Republican John McCain's thirty-two percent.[20]

Migrants and Welfare

In 1882, Congress passed legislation prohibiting the admission of immigrants who were "likely to become a public charge." Later the law was amended to allow for the removal of anyone who became a public charge within two years after entering the country. Neither law has ever been seriously enforced.

The eligibility for public assistance has varied through history, as have its definitions. Most people would agree that Aid to Families with Dependent Children (AFDC), Supplemental Security Income (SSI), Food Stamps, Temporary Assistance to Needy Families (TANF), Medicaid, Women, Infants, and Children (WIC), Head Start, and Section 8 Housing Assistance are "welfare" programs.

In the absence of factual information about migrant usage of entitlement programs and related issues, the mood of the country got ugly following the 1994 passage of Proposition 187 in California. Governor Pete Wilson even issued a call to reject the Fourteenth Amendment and deny citizenship to U.S.-born children of undocumented parents, eliminating them from eligibility for WIC and Medicaid. Members of California's congressional delegation in Washington introduced a similar bill, which went nowhere, and Proposition 187 was overturned before it was enacted. An effort in 2011 saw five states led by Arizona attempting to cancel U.S. citizenship for children born of parents who are here illegally. An important difference between this and earlier attempts is that the language seeks to "cancel" citizenship already obtained instead of not conferring it in the first place.

Despite sensationalism to the contrary, most means tested, or "unearned" government benefits are not even available to *legal* immigrants who came here after 1996, although President Bush did restore food stamps to legal permanent residents in 2003. Restoring this benefit to LPRs was influenced by the fact that these benefits were already available to refugees and asylees, and the action was also influenced by the upcoming elections in 2004. The new law did not apply to pre-1996 immigrants who were already receiving assistance from the federal government.[21]

The 1996 law ruled that *indocumentados* were ineligible for any form of federal assistance except for Medicaid, administered through the states, and only on an emergency basis. "Emergency" is variously defined as a patient showing up at an emergency room instead of making an appointment, someone who has a condition that will lead to death if not treated immediately, or various standards in between. Follow-up care for a brief period may also be covered. The cost of such treatment is usually split fifty-fifty between the state and the federal government.

The law left the door open for states to offer their own safety net to migrants, and many states where a migrant presence is critical to their economy do offer some relief. Critics of migrant welfare who think they are discussing federal welfare programs are often confusing them with state programs. For the most part, stories about migrants abusing the system are unproven or exaggerated.

Nevertheless, in *State of Emergency*, Patrick Buchanan quotes Dr. Madeleine Cosman in the spring 2005 issue of the *American Physicians and Surgeons* as saying, "Illegal alien women come to the hospital in labor and drop their little anchors, each of whom pulls its illegal alien mother, father, and siblings into permanent residency simply by being born within our borders. Anchor babies are citizens, and instantly qualify for public welfare aid."[22]

Buchanan went on to say, "Mostly uneducated and poor, [migrants] get more back in government benefits — free education for their children, housing subsidies, free health care, food stamps, welfare checks, Supplemental Security Income, [and] earned income tax credits."[23] The statement is worse than untrue and Buchanan had to know it.

It is true that about one in twelve babies born in the United States is born of a non-citizen mother.[24] However, as to bringing the rest of the family into permanent residency, the family will have to wait until the "anchor," turns twenty-one so that he or she can legally petition the federal government for family reunification. If the "anchor baby" is Mexican, the legal wait time could be more than a decade (see Chapter Three).

Notes

1 William R. Wynn, "National Anthem in Spanish has Historic Roots," *La Semana del Sur*, 2-8 Jul 2006: A1, A 3.

2 Ruben G. Rumbaut and Walter A. Ewing, "The Myth of Immigrant Criminality and the Paradox of Assimilation: Incarceration Rates among Native and Foreign-Born Men," *Special Report*, Immigration Policy Center, a division of the American Immigration Law Foundation (Washington: Spring 2007) 2, 11. Rumbaut did not report an increase in divorce, although other authors have.

3 California UP, *Mexus News* (Winter 1999).

4 The interaction between two cultures in a borderlands area has become a specialized field of study where students can earn advanced degrees.

5 Miriam Jordan, "Illegal Residents Get Legal Route to Car Coverage: Insurers Find a Market as States Crack Down on Driver's Licenses," *Wall Street Journal*, 1 May 2007: A 11.

6 Jordan, "Illegal Residents."

7 Haya El Nasser, "Immigrants Turn Utah into Mini-Melting Pot," *USA Today*, 15 Sep 2006: 1A.

8 Jacob Gershman, "Spitzer Poised to Ease Access to Licenses," *The New York Sun*, 19 Jan 2007, 21 Dec 2007 <www.nysun.com/article/46973>.

9 Jordan, "Illegal Residents," A-1.

10 Raul Lowery Contreras, *The New American Majority: Hispanics, Republicans, and George Bush* (San Jose: Writer's Showcase, 2002), 40.

11 Deborah Solomon, "Test of Faith," *Wall Street Journal*, 10-11 Jun 2006: A 4.

12 Cross-denominational comparisons are difficult because the Catholic Church counts anyone who was ever baptized in the faith, irrespective of their current affiliation.

13 "Now Pentecostalism is Able to Draw Guatemala's Poorest," *Wall Street Journal*, 18 Dec 2007: B 10, quoting the *Christian Science Monitor*.

14 Richard Rodriquez, *Days of Obligation: An Argument with My Mexican Father* (New York: Penguin, 1992), 176.

15 Rodriquez, *Days of Obligation*.

16 PEW Center Advisory, "Changing Faiths: Latinos and the Transformation of American Religion," 25 Apr 2007 <www.pewhispanic.org>.

17 Susan Page, "Hispanics are returning to Democrats for 2008," *USA Today*, 28 Jun 2007: A 4.

18 PEW Center Press Release, "PEW Center Releases Report on the Hispanic Vote in the Presidential Election," 5 Nov 2008, 11 Nov 2008 <www.pewhispanic.org>.

19 Kathy Kiely, "Republicans Lose Ground among Hispanic Voters," *USA Today*, 11 Sep 2006, 3 Jun 2007 <www.usatoday.com/news/politicselections/vote>.

20 Julia Preston, "In Big Shift, Latino Vote Was Heavily for Obama," *The New York Times*, 11 Nov 2008, 3 Jun 2009 <www.nytime.com2008/11/07/us/politics/07latino>.

21 T. Alexander Aleinikoff, "Between Principles and Politics: United States Citizenship Policy," *From Migrants to Citizens: Membership in a Changing World*, Eds. T. Alexander Aleinikoff and Douglas Klusmeyer (Washington: Carnegie Endowment for International Peace, 2000), 131.

22 Patrick J. Buchanan, *State of Emergency: the Third World Invasion and Conquest of America* (New York: Thomas Dunne-St. Martins Press, 2006), 31.

23 Buchanan, *State of Emergency*, 60.

24 Arthur Brice, "Report: 8 Percent of U.S. Newborn Have Undocumented Parents," *CNNUS*, 8 August 2010, 22 August 2010 <http://cnn.com2010US0811hispanic.study/index.html?e>.

Chapter Eight

Photo Credit: Vincent Blaine

> *It's like there are two signs on the border, 'Help Wanted' and 'Keep Out.'*
> Ruben Navarette[1]

THE ECONOMY

Coyotes

HISPANIC MALES REPORTEDLY have the highest workforce participation of any statistical group in the United States.[2] Most studies agree that they add ten percent or more to the U.S. economy each year.

However, other sources suggest that they create a loss of about ten percent because of their alleged abuse of welfare programs and medical services.

Conventional wisdom is that migrants come to the United States seeking work, and this is the case most of the time. However, some migrants already have work lined up, and "sell" their old job back home to help pay for their border crossing with a crossing guide, or *coyote*.

Consider the case of an undocumented teenager from Guatemala who used a coyote to cross the border in 2002. The price was $1,600.00. How does a peasant in Guatemala come up with that kind of money? "The first time I borrowed the money from relatives, but I got deported a year later," he said. "In 2006, I decided to come back with my brother-in-law and my cousin. By then, the coyote wanted $2,000.00 apiece. I called my old boss in Arkansas and he wired us $6,000.00."

Migrants and their employers are willing to pay these high fees. What does this say about the U.S. labor market?

In the past, the coyote's fee was only for crossing the border. Now the contract is usually for a portal-to-portal experience, and the coyote is not paid until the migrant has arrived safely at his final destination.[3] Migrants do not carry cash on their journey for the same reason they do not carry identification (see Chapter One). Upon arrival, the coyote will be paid by a friend, relative, or employer.

The exception to this is when a border crosser attempts to make a "look alike" run. In this case, the migrant chooses an I-94 Work Authorization from of a selection provided by the coyote. If the attempt is successful, a confederate returns the document later.

The coyote's fee reflects beefed-up efforts to secure the border by the U.S. Border Patrol, bribes for the Mexican Federal Police (*los Federales*), and military units operating near the border. Even after these expenses, a good coyote can earn $60,000.00 per year.[4]

If caught north of the border, a coyote faces a charge of trafficking in human cargo, which comes with a lengthy prison term since trafficking is a human rights violation under America law. American citizens account for a high percentage of the trafficking charges. In the mid-nineteenth century, Harriet Tubman provided the same services, but the U.S. government has honored her by putting her likeness on a postage stamp.

Dying to Work

Some migrants are literally dying to work. A senior border patrol official said, "The idea was if we seal off the urban areas, we're going to force them into the desert, and the desert is inhospitable; they're not going to go there."[5] San Diego, California, and Nogales, Arizona, are two urban areas where border patrol practices have forced migrants into the desert. When enhanced enforcement went into effect in 1993, apprehensions of undocumented migrants along Arizona's 375-mile long border with Mexico were only nine percent of the nation's total. A year later, the figure was fifty-one percent.[6]

The border patrol's policy for the new millennium is essentially a shell game that pushes border crossers away from high visibility urban areas where residents have political influence to rural areas where the individual residents are less powerful.[7] The idea is also to keep the crossers from being able to blend into city crowds. Despite favorable publicity on operations with catchy names like Operation Wetback, Hold-the-Line, Gatekeeper, Blockade, Safeguard, and Rio Grande, illegal migration has not declined.[8]

A retired border patrol supervisor said, "They're still coming. You have to understand what the border patrol does. When it makes a lot of arrests, it claims success for making a lot of arrests. When it doesn't make a lot of arrests, it also claims success because . . . there are fewer crossings. No matter what happens, it declares victory."[9] "The United States arrests enough of the border crossers to create the illusion that it is enforcing immigration laws while allowing the great majority to get through."[10] The border patrol has also been accused of inflating its arrest numbers to get more funding out of Washington, then deflating them to look successful.[11]

Meier and Ribera wrote, "Statistics on Mexican immigration are important, but they must be used with great caution, for they can only indicate general trends."[12] For instance, if the border patrol apprehends the same person three or four times in one week, their reporting will show that they apprehended three or four different people, not one person.

The new policies for protecting the border have increased the danger of border crossing for migrants, but for most, it is a risk is worth taking. Even so, scores of *indocumentados* drown each year trying to cross the Rio Grande (*Rio Bravo*), or die in the deserts. Border patrol agents say that the desert is by far the riskier of the two.[13]

The number of known border crossing deaths appears to be about five hundred per year, with the probability of a similar number of unreported deaths. Many of the deceased are not identified, and their families never know the fate of their loved ones. Migrants face other dangers. By the time they get across the border, they may have been beaten, extorted, or sexually molested by criminals or Mexican authorities.[14]

It may come as a surprise to Americans who hear about vigilante groups patrolling the border, but there are numerous humanitarian groups working there also, usually affiliated with mainline churches.[15] Volunteers stock well-marked water stations for border crossers and sometimes provide medical assistance. In areas without water stations, migrants may resort to drinking their own urine or drinking out of pesticide laden irrigation ditches.

The Pima County, Arizona Board of Supervisors once voted to give one local organization $25,000.00 for humanitarian relief.[16] This organization has placed over one hundred large water barrels on trails known to be used by migrants crossing the border. They also report that sometimes these water stations have been vandalized by local residents or removed by the border patrol.[17]

At one time, border patrol officers had reportedly agreed to ignore migrants discovered at the water stations maintained by the humanitarian groups, but the current status of this agreement is unclear.[18] What is clear is that beginning in 2008, border patrol officers in Arizona began issuing citations for "littering" to volunteers placing water barrels on the migrant trails.

These cases must be heard in federal court. The maximum penalty is one year in jail and/or a $100,000 fine. The organizations argue that thousands of migrants have died in the past decade and that giving water to a dying person when the temperature is over one hundred degrees is providing emergency medical care, and should not be against the law.[19]

Since the creation of the U.S. Border Patrol in 1924, humanitarian efforts by the border patrol have saved thousands of lives. In fact, the border patrol operates a highly trained, albeit controversial search and rescue division known as BORSTAR. Since the border patrol's inception, one hundred thirteen agents have died in the line of duty, including three women agents.[20] Employees of the U.S. Fish and Wildlife Service and the Bureau of Land Management have also saved the lives of many migrants at great risk to themselves.[21]

One unplanned result of forcing border crossers into the deserts is litter. Unlike the permanent environmental damage associated with the *maquiladoras* (see Chapter Ten), litter can be cleaned up. Environmental groups claim that this will cost millions of dollars. In fact, the government could use its alien detainees and the high traffic areas could be cleaned up in a month for next to nothing. In Wisconsin, state agencies have been using inmate labor since Governor Scott Walker gutted the state's collective bargaining rights for labor unions.[22] The federal government should seriously consider some similar solution.

"They're Here to Take Our Jobs"

There are two labor markets in any economy. The primary market consists of jobs that pay well, offer prestige, benefits, opportunities for advancement, and job security for better-educated workers. The secondary market is characterized by low wages, unstable employment, no benefits, and little prospect for advancement.

Historically, women, minorities, and teenagers have filled jobs in the secondary market. However, equal opportunity laws have moved women and minorities into the primary market, including some who don't belong there, and America's low birth rate has reduced the supply of teenagers.

The unintended effect has been to create more employment opportunities at the bottom, especially for undocumented workers.

Nativists say that migrants, especially Mexicans, steal jobs that are needed by native-born workers or cause jobs to be relocated overseas. However, migrants do not cause jobs to be outsourced—only employers can do that. Migrants cause jobs to stay here. The results of migrant labor (new home construction, consumer goods, etc.) are here to be purchased, used, and taxed.

The idea that every employed migrant is taking a job from a native-born citizen is not true, and it is over-worked to say that migrants take jobs that American citizens do not want. Migrants take jobs that American citizens do not want to be *seen* doing, even if the wages are reasonable. Migrants help the economy to expand, and that expansion leads to job opportunities at higher levels and higher salaries more suited to unemployed, native-born American workers.

Blacks, like nativists, are especially negative about Mexican immigration, which is ironic since it was the late Barbara Jordan, a black U.S. Representative from Texas, who first lobbied to have Hispanics added to existing civil rights legislation in the 1970s.[23]

Blacks were not adversely affected by Asian migration at the conclusion of the Vietnam War in 1975. The Vietnamese, like other Asians, assimilated quickly, and blacks remained the nation's largest minority. Blacks were not threatened by Cubans from the Mariel Boat Lift in 1994, or a second wave of Cuban *balseros* in 1998. Along with most Americans, blacks were not happy about the benefits bestowed upon the Cubans although many of the Cubans were black (see Chapter One). Still, blacks remained the dominant minority.[24]

However, blacks are vehement about the current crop of Hispanics, who they blame for so many blacks being at the bottom of society. Before the current Hispanic migration blacks had high rates of unemployment and incarceration so their logic does not hold up. (In 2007, the imprisonment rate of black males was 6.5 times higher than white males and 2.5 higher than Hispanic males.)[25]

Nathan Glazer referred to this as "the continued presence of what appears to be an almost permanent caste composed of the black race."[26]

Peter Brimelow wrote, "It would appear that public policy is subsidizing their [blacks] choosiness about work, thus artificially stimulating the demand for immigrants."[27]

Blacks are not the only ones who are choosy. U.S. Senator Diane Feinstein told of a help-wanted ad placed for agricultural workers in fifty-eight California newspapers to which not one U.S. citizen applied.[28] U.S. citizens who claim that migrants take American jobs would be hard pressed to name someone they personally know who has actually lost a job to a migrant.

Who, then, is being counted in this cohort of U.S. citizens allegedly unemployed due to migrant labor? U.S. workers experienced periodic unemployment long before Mexican and Central American workers arrived—blacks, historically, and others for various reasons. Some people may be temporarily out of the workforce due to illness; some may be disabled. Some workers may not be able to get back and forth to work because they don't drive and mass transit is unavailable in their community. Some people are incarcerated. Some are in school. Some are in the military. Some are retired.

Many American teenagers will not cross the street for a job, and were ill prepared for the world of work either at home or at school. They may live off their parents, or they may find street life (crime, drugs, or gangs) more to their liking. Lazy or perpetually unemployed native-born citizens are more problematic to the American economy than migrants who work.

Whoever the unemployed are, they are disinclined to eviscerate a chicken, or perform stoop labor. Many politicians and talk show hosts blame the U.S. unemployment problem on Hispanic migrants for taking those jobs, but who would take them otherwise?

Of the native-born unemployed, how many would move to a border state to perform stoop labor? How many Americans could *afford* a move to another state if they were unemployed? Would their home state terminate their unemployment benefits if they refused to relocate for such a job?

Migrants may relocate to follow harvest patterns or construction trends or just for the opportunity to work outside of a border state. They used to be better paid than their *comprades* who stayed in the border states due to a phenomenon know as "further-higher." That is, the further north a migrant went, the higher wages would be. However, as employment of migrants has become geographically diverse, "further-higher" has assumed less importance.

Americans need to understand that having a strong economy is nothing to be ashamed of, and that it will encourage migration, both legal and illegal. At a minimum, migrants represent new consumers and the potential for more taxpayers. They will create demand for more products and services, in turn creating more jobs.

Undocumented migrants are filling large numbers of McJobs at the bottom of the economic ladder. One complaint is that they drive wages down for workers in general, which is not true, although they may drive wages down for other migrants, especially the newly arrived.[29]

Migrant wages are generally lower than wages for the native-born because migrants have fewer job skills, little education or English language skills, no transportation and no back-up network. How can such a marginal person pose a threat to a native-born citizen who possesses all of these attributes plus years of experience in the American free enterprise system?

Many undocumented workers work in substandard conditions for employers who offer sub-minimum wages. It is with these workers where the potential for abuse is the greatest. Their employers may falsely claim deductions for health insurance, FICA, worker's compensation, and Social Security. In this case, it is the employer who is "illegal," but the undocumented worker is not in a position to report the abuse. In day labor and agriculture an employer who uses a labor broker (*contratista*) is absolved of liability. Although potentially liable, labor brokers are not well capitalized and generally have no fixed assets.[30]

The lowest paid workers are undocumented, unskilled laborers employed as domestics or in agribusiness, lodging, or food service. It is axiomatic that labor intensive jobs in low tech businesses will always go to low wage workers. Businesses that do not need highly skilled or well-educated workers have no reason to hire them if a less costly alternative is available.

Migrants do tend to cluster in professional groups after arriving in the United States. Landscaping, housekeeping, meatpacking, food service, and construction are heavily Hispanic. Koreans are well represented in building maintenance as are Filipinos in health care. Immigrants from India and Pakistan have been successful in the lodging industry and operating small retail establishments. Other groups dominate in other sectors. If the United States heeds the call of Americans who want mass removals of undocumented workers, large sectors of the economy could collapse, especially in Texas, California, and New York.

Quality of work and dependability are as important to American business as low wages are. Carlos Fuentes wrote, "If low wages were the principal factor in attracting jobs, Bangladesh would be an employment paradise...It is not."[31]

An owner of a lawn service said, "If a blade gets dull on a lawn mower being operated by an American kid, he won't do anything about it. A Mexican will pull a file out of his back pocket, sharpen the blade, and go back to work. Also, Mexicans aren't always making excuses about why they can't get to work on time, or why they need the day off. I treat them well, and they are not poorly paid. And my jobs can't be shipped overseas."

Cash or Credit?

Hispanics have been exposed to American products all of their lives. North of the border, recognition of Hispanic buying power is evidenced by aggressive marketing from companies like Ace Hardware, Colgate, Nescafe, Kraft, U.S. Sprint, Home Depot, Wal-Mart, Blue Cross and Blue Shield in many states, and thousands of other companies.[32]

Until recently, Hispanics have thought that mainstream financial services were out of reach to them. However, all a bank needs to open a checking account is proof of residency, and some reasonable form of identification. For Mexicans, a *Matricula Consular* is generally enough (see Chapter Six). A Social Security number is *not* required to open a bank account. Some banks actually provide a Social Security Form W-7 that the applicant can mail to the IRS to receive an individual taxpayer identification number (ITIN), even if that person is undocumented. To their credit, the IRS tries to collect taxes even if the individual is not working here legally. However, the IRS does not share information with law enforcement agencies, creating a conflict between tax law and immigration law.

ITINs were created in 1996 to provide resident and non-resident aliens who are not eligible to obtain a Social Security card with an identification number for tax purposes. ITINs do *not* change a person's immigration status, allow them to work legally, or entitle them to Social Security benefits.

In recent years, some illegal workers have not only filed but over-paid their taxes in order to improve their standing with the government in the event of legal problems or another amnesty. From 1996 to 2003, the income tax liability for those filers was almost $50 billion dollars.[33] By 2007, over 1.8 million undocumented taxpayers felt safe in filing their taxes with an ITIN instead of a Social Security Number, a two hundred forty six percent increase over 2002.[34] The idea of an illegal worker receiving a tax refund goes against the grain for many U.S. citizens, and some have called for a surcharge on these refunds if they are to continue.[35]

Most migrants have never dealt with a bank or a credit card company. Instead, they carry cash, making them prime targets for criminals. Bank of America and CitiGroup have both offered debit or credit cards to undocumented workers who lack a Social Security number and credit history, and Wells Fargo is reported to be considering such a move. It is illegal to employ undocumented workers, but it is not illegal to have them as customers.[36] The high interest plastic that these banks issue are usually linked to a checking or savings account or come with a high up-front fee.

Two big lenders offer mortgages to consumers using only an individual taxpayer identification number. Second Federal Savings of Chicago has over $90 million dollars on loan in this way.[37] Wells Fargo has been making mortgage loans based on ITINs since 2005.[38]

Remittances

Americans regularly hear stories about large numbers of Hispanics living together in close quarters in order to economize. For the most part, these stories are exaggerated. However, to the degree that the stories may be true, the practice does help migrants save so they can send money to their families, often $500.00 or more per month. According to *The Washington Post*, Mexican citizens working in the United States sent home $24.2 billion dollars in 2006.[39] That amount is equal to Mexico's total oil revenues, and greater than its tourist income.[40] Western Union and other wire transfer companies charge fees that are in the billions of dollars per year, a fact that has become a flash point for some Hispanic organizations.[41]

The U.S. Federal Reserve's automated clearinghouse is linked to *Banco de Mexico* and member banks in the United States can offer fast, inexpensive, and safe transfer services. Participating banks charge as little as $2.50 per transfer compared to as much as $40.00 charged by private sector firms.[42]

Remittances are directly tied to the health of the U.S. economy, especially to the housing industry.[43] Mexico relies heavily on these remittances, and much Mexican development is remittance-based.

Nativists object to seeing American dollars leaving the community, even though virtually all money leaves a community at some point. After a migrant worker is paid, he may purchase clothes, make a payment on his vehicle, get a haircut, buy groceries, or pay rent. Employees at the businesses where the migrant trades will also get a paycheck and they will make purchases in their community with their earnings. The money from these transactions turns repeatedly in the community. What is important is not that money eventually leaves the country but how many times it turns before leaving. Even some of the money that migrants send to their family will be spent on American-made goods there.

The money that migrants send home helps their families and their communities. Mexicans working in an American community often come from the same village or region. In the past, construction workers took off during the winter months when construction work in the United States was slow. To encourage community development, some Mexican states match money pooled by their expatriate citizens working in the United States three to one.[44] While visiting home, the men might use these funds to work on a community project, such as adding a room to a school, or digging a new well. When people do things for themselves with their own money, the United States will spend less on foreign aid. However, the increased difficulty and expense of returning to the United States has brought this practice to a standstill. The worldwide economic downturn since 2008 has caused remittances to drop precipitously. However remittances were substantially higher at the beginning of 2011 than they were at the beginning of 2010, which may signal some economic recovery in the U.S.[45]

Notes

1 Ruben Navarette, "Can You Make it Past my Last Name?" *CNN*, 24 Aug 2006, 23 Nov 2007 <http://www.cnn.worldnews>.

2 Michael Barone, "Back into the Melting Pot: The Welcome Effects of Latino Immigration," *The Weekly Standard*, 6-13 Jul 1998: 30. Barone quotes Roberto Suro from *Strangers Among Us*.

3 Terry McCarthy, "The Coyote's Game," *Time*, 11 Jun 2001: 60.

4 Peter Andreas, "The Escalation of Immigration Control," *Border Games: Policing the United States-Mexico Divide* (Ithaca: Cornell University Press, 2000), 96.

5 Brenda Rodriquez, "Border Desperation," *Dallas Morning News*, 1 Jul 2001: 1A.

6 Donald L. Bartlett and James B. Steele, "Who Left the Door Open?" *Time*, 20 Sep 2004: 54.

7 John J. Miller, "Border Blues: They Keep Coming and Coming, and Citizens Are at Wit's End," *National Review*, 14 March 2002: 41.

8 Miller, "Border Blues."

9 Miller, "Border Blues," 43.

10 Bartlett, "Who Left the Door Open?" 54.

11 Sebastian Rotella, *Twilight on the Line: Underworlds and Politics at the U.S.-Mexican Border* (New York: W. W. Norton, 1998), 32.

12 Matt A. Meier and Feliciano Ribera, *Mexican Americans/American Mexicans: From Conquistadors to Chicanos* (New York: Hill and Wang-Farrar Straus & Giroux, 1972), 127.

13 Rodriquez, "Border Desperation," 18A.

14 Earl Shorris, *Latinos* (New York: Norton, 1992), 270.

15 The U.S. Border Patrol is the only American law enforcement agency that tolerates or encourages the participation of vigilantes.

16 Laurie Goodstein, "Church Group Provides Oasis for Illegal Migrants to United States," *The New York Times*, 10 Jul 2001: 20.

17 "Feds Hand Out 13 Littering Tickets," News Updates, *No More Deaths.*

18 Rodriquez, "Border Desperation," 20A.

19 Rodriquez, "Border Desperation," 20A.

20 United States. Customs and Border Patrol, Border Patrol and Agent Memorial, (Washington GPO: 2010) <http://www.cbp.gov/xp/cgw/border_security_borderpatrol_borderpatrolmemorial>. Two additional deaths occurred in the spring of 2011 changing the total to one hundred thirteen.

21 Rodriquez, "Border Desperation," 18A.

22 "Wis. Uses Inmate for Gov't Work," *Politico,* 7 July 2011 <http://dyn/politico.com/printstoru.cfm?uuid-63CD568E-F-1...>

23 Michael Barone, "Back into the Melting Pot: The Welcome Effects of Latino Immigration," *The Weekly Standard,* 6-13 July 1998: 30.

24 Roger Daniels, *Coming to America: A History of Immigration and Ethnicity in American Life,* 2nd ed. (New York: Perennial-HarperCollins, 2002), 376.

25 United States. U.S. Department of Justice, Bureau of Prison Statistics, Office of Justice Programs, *Prisoners in 2007* NCJ224280 by Heather C. West and William J. Sabol (Washington: GPO, 2008), 4.

26 Nathan Glazer, "American Diversity and the 2000 Census," *The Public Interest* 144 (2001): 3.

27 Peter Brimelow, "Time to Rethink Immigration," *Immigration: Debating the Issues* Ed. Nicholas Capaldi (Amherst: Prometheus, 1997), 48. The parenthetical interpretation is mine.

28 "Statement of Senator Diane Feinstein Urging Support for Comprehensive Immigration Proposal," *California Chronicle,* 30 Mar 2006, 7 Jan 2008 <http://www.californiachronicle.com/articles/viewArticle>.

29 Roberto Suro, *Strangers Among Us: Latino Lives in a Changing America* (New York: Vintage-Random House, 1999), 278.

30 Kevin O'Leary, "Fatal Sunshine: The Plight of California's Farm Workers," *Time,* 9 Aug 2009 <http://www.time.com/nation/article/0,8599,1914961,00html>.

31 Carlos Fuentes, *A New Time for Mexico* (Berkeley: California UP, 1997), 161.

32 Brian Grow, "Embracing Illegals: Companies Are Getting Hooked on the Buying Power of 11 Million Undocumented Immigrants," *Business Week*, 18 Jul 2005: 59.

33 Grow, "Embracing Illegals," 58.

34 United States. U.S. Treasury, Memo for Commissioner, Wage and Investment Division by Michael R. Phillips (Washington GPO: 2009).

35 Grow, "Embracing Illegals," 59.

36 Miriam Jordan, "Bank of America Casts Wider Net for Hispanics: Lender Risks Controversy Aiming New Credit Card at Illegal Immigrants," *Wall Street Journal*, 14 Feb 2007: A-23.

37 "Even Workers in United States Illegally Pay Tax Man," *Wall Street Journal*, 4 Apr 2007: B-12.

38 Shaffer Page, Letter, *Wall Street Journal*, 13 Apr 2007: A-11.

39 Karin Broulliard, "Migrants Sent Home $300 Billion in 2006," *Washington Post*, 17 Oct 2007, 18 Oct 2007 <http://www.washingtonpost.com/wp-dyn/content/article>.

40 "Give and Take Across the Border: 1 in 7 Mexican Workers Migrates-Most Send Money Home," *San Francisco Chronicle*, 21 May 2006 <http://www.sfgate.com/cgi-bin/article.cgi>.

41 "Immigrants Target Money Transfer-Industry," *La Semana del Sur*, 23-29 September: A-6.

42 Miriam Jordan, "U.S. Banks Woo Migrants, Legal or Otherwise," *Wall Street Journal*, 11 Oct 2006: B1, B2.

43 Joel Millman, "Latin America Feels Pain of U.S. Housing Slump," *Wall Street Journal*, 23 Apr 2007: A2.

44 Nancy Gibbs, "A Whole New World," *Time*, 11 Jun 2001: 60.

45 Miriam Jordan and Paulo Trevisani, "Buoyed by Recovery, Migrants Send Home More Money," *Wall Street Journal*, 14 March 2011 <http://online.wsj.com/article/SB10001424052748704027500>.

Photo Credit: Vincent Blaine

Chapter Nine

NAFTA

Trading Blocs

ANY DISCUSSION OF North American migration must acknowledge the related effects of NAFTA.

In the late 1980s, Brazil and Chile spearheaded an effort to organize Central and South American countries into a cohesive trading bloc. By 1991, the Common Market of the South, or MERCOSUR, was composed of Argentina, Bolivia, Brazil, Chile, Colombia, Costa Rica, the Dominican Republic, and Venezuela.1 More recently, the Dominican Republic, El Salvador, Guatemala, Honduras, Nicaragua, and Peru have organized themselves in the Central American Free Trade Association (CAFTA.)

Mexico has always perceived its situation and its needs to be different from that of its neighbors. Initially, Mexico's Harvard educated President Carlos Salinas de Gortari tried to attract large-scale investment from Europe and Japan. When that failed, he decided that an economic association with the United States would yield greater benefits than membership in MERCOSUR, giving Mexico advantage and status over the rest of the Americas.2

It is difficult to decide whether Mexico is a first or second world country, a developed or developing nation. Even prior to NAFTA, Mexico had the thirteenth largest economy in the world, and yielded a high number of billionaires for its population.3 On that basis Mexico was a first world, developed nation, but based on its poverty and outflow of migrant labor, Mexico was a second world country. Prior to NAFTA, one-third of Mexico's population lived in poverty.4 One half never finished the six grade, and unemployment was high.5

In 1990, the Salinas government began formal negotiations with the administration of George H. W. Bush on an idea originally proposed by then California Governor Jerry Brown in 1979.[6] This idea became known as the North American Free Trade Agreement, or NAFTA. In Mexico, NAFTA was opposed by the influential newspaper, *El Financiero*.[7] In the United States, NAFTA was opposed by AFL-CIO.[8]

After Canada joined the United States and Mexico, NAFTA represented 370 million people compared to 500 million people for the European Union. NAFTA represented a combined economic output of six trillion dollars annually.[9] Congress approved NAFTA in November 1993, and it became law on January 1, 1994 with the signature of the newly inaugurated President Clinton.

Clinton haters on the far right still refer to the agreement as "William Jefferson Clinton's NAFTA," using the former President's middle name as a parent would with an errant child. The irony is that NAFTA was a Republican initiative belonging to Clinton's predecessor. Early in the campaign, Clinton was lukewarm to the proposal, but he supported it once there were provisions for environmental safeguards and workers rights.[10] He signed the legislation into law when it was presented to him as president, but he did not originate it.

Mexico, the United States, and Canada have always had substantial commerce with one another. NAFTA was to eliminate tariffs, duties, and other trade barriers between the three countries over a fifteen-year period, and open up the borders to a free flow of products, services, and capital.[11] However, as former Mexican President Vicente Fox and others have pointed out, beyond a new category of visas for corporate executives and highly skilled professionals, NAFTA made no provision for the free flow of labor.[12]

Carlos Salinas' vision was to export tomatoes, but Mexico continues to export tomato pickers.[13] NAFTA created a borderless economy, albeit a barricaded border. Fox's call for open borders was never well received in the United States, and he dropped the subject after the terrorist attack in the United States on September 11, 2001.[14]

Carlos Fuentes wrote, "In the past, Mexico got pneumonia when the United States caught a cold, today we get the flu together.[15] Both American and Mexican economists have envisioned that NAFTA could be a common vaccine which might one day resemble the European Common Market's

Eurodollar approach. The idea would allow the three neighbors to prosper together, instead of at one another's expense, and to do so without the problem of fluctuating currencies. Having an entire hemisphere locked into a major trade agreement also makes the weaker members less likely to stray from the strongest one on issues of diplomacy and defense.

Mexico's alignment with two advanced technological powers, one of them the undisputed leader of the First World, positioned it to attract the foreign capital that it originally sought. Mexican exports to the United States have continued to increase since NAFTA was signed in 1994. By 2002, the United States was consuming ninety percent of Mexico's exports. Mexico is one of the three largest trading partners of the United States, bigger than Japan, and bigger than France, Germany, Great Britain, and Italy combined.[16]

Since tariffs were already low between the three nations, "free trade" was never a real issue for the United States. Noam Chomsky suggested that NAFTA was highly protectionist, and designed to thwart East Asian and European competitors.[17] NAFTA also left the United States better positioned for future access to Mexico's offshore oil, and more importantly, for continued access to Mexico's most valuable export, low-income workers.[18]

NAFTA was trumpeted as being good for northern Mexico's borderlands area. It did not prove to be good for Mexico's south.[19] The fact that southern Mexico did not reap any benefits from NAFTA was one of the complaints in Mexico's Chiapas uprising. Ultimately, however, NAFTA did not prove to be very good for Mexico's north, either.

Maquiladoras

At the end of the *Bracero* Program in 1964, Mexico initiated the Border Industrialization Program (BIP). Its aim was to find work for the *bracero* farm workers who had been exiled from the United States and to keep them working on Mexican soil.[20]

In stages, Mexico and the United States agreed on a fifty-two mile wide Foreign Trade Zone (FTZ) in the *Zona Norte* where the United

States could send raw materials or parts to assembly plants, called *maquiladoras*, to be processed or assembled in Mexican facilities, then shipped back to the United States for final finishing before sale.[21] The American products are not sold in or to Mexico, but held "in bond," avoiding entry and exit fees, and they are only taxed on the value added to the product while it is in Mexico. For American businessmen, the maquiladoras are also a way to avoid environmental regulations in the United States and keep costs down without having to pay for restrictive environmental technology.

Prior to NAFTA, there were approximately three hundred *maquiladoras* in Mexico, most on the outskirts of San Diego / Tijuana, El Paso / Juarez, and Brownsville / Matamoras. Today, there are easily five thousand *maquiladoras* housing corporate giants like Sony, RCA, Honda, JVC, Mitsubishi, Samsung, Nissan, National Cash Register, Honeywell, TDK, General Motors, IBM, Rockwell, Kodak, Memorex, Goodyear, Kimberly-Clark, Sanyo, Hitachi, Panasonic, Zenith, Pioneer, IBM, Canon, Hewlett Packard, and General Electric.[22] Even businesses that eventually relocate to Mexico because of NAFTA still strengthen the strategic position of the United States in comparison to the other two great trading blocs, Asia and Europe.[23]

Most *Maquiladoras* are now located in the Mexican border states of Baja California, Sonora, Chihuahua, Coahuila, Nuevo Leon, and Tamaulipas.[24] Some of the plants employ as many as fifteen thousand workers.[25] Additionally, there are many dependent businesses related to the *maquiladoras*. These factors swell the economic and political importance of the *Zona Norte*.

At first, many Fortune 500 companies thought they could run the maquiladoras themselves.[26] However, for legal and practical reasons, these enterprises were soon turned over to the Mexicans. Now, over ninety percent of the maquiladoras are controlled by foreign capital, largely Japanese and Middle Eastern, and U.S. companies only have the use of them.

Directly or indirectly, the FTZ helps to support millions of people.[27] However, millions of people are just a fraction of the Mexican population, and most of the revenue from the *maquiladoras* is taken by the central government to Mexico City instead of being allowed to remain in the originating states.

Rather than hiring the *braceros* as originally planned, the *maquiladoras* now hire women almost exclusively – Mexico's version of "Rosie the Riveter."[28] In a typical *maquiladora*, the wages are so low and conditions are so bad that employee turnover runs one hundred to three hundred percent per year.[29] Other than low wage employment for some of its citizens, Mexico profits little from this system. The *maquiladoras* are foreign owned and the output is exported tax and duty free.[30]

In northern Mexico, change from the *maquiladoras* has not only been rapid, it has been extreme. Sprawling shantytowns exist where housing is at a premium, rent is high, and workers are often crammed into quarters less desirable than the homes they left behind. Extortion ("taxation") is commonplace. Substance abuse and abortions are high. Violent crime is rampant, and hundreds of female *maquiladora* workers have been murdered since the 1990s.[31]

Municipal infrastructures in the FTZ are stressed and public utilities are inadequate.[32] The water table has dropped dangerously in the bioregion, and most of the water is polluted by the manufacturing processes of the *maquiladoras*. American entrepreneurs profit by trucking potable water into Mexico and selling it at a premium.

The FTZ is good for the United States; it is not so good for Mexico. Access to capital and the means of production are still not available to the average Mexican. The descendants of the *braceros* still line up at dusk for their illegal trip across the border in order to earn money in the United States. They cannot support their families in the Mexican economy, NAFTA or not.

Workers are not the only thing leaving Mexico. While three-quarters of the world's *maquiladoras* are located along the 1,957 mile long U.S.-Mexican border, some *maquiladoras* are relocating to other parts of Mexico where land and labor are cheaper yet.[33] Some companies have relocated to China or other countries where prison labor is considered a qualified work force.[34]

For better or worse, NAFTA and the *maquiladoras* have transformed northern Mexico ecologically, economically, and politically. What is troubling is the American hand in this. Had the United States exercised higher standards (i.e., "would we do this to our own citizens?") the situation along the border would be very different.

Organized Labor

Union membership in the United States has fallen from just under 30 percent of the workforce in 1955 to approximately ten percent of the workforce today.[35] Unions have kept their hold on key industries like transportation and communication, although their influence has been steadily weakening. Since 1979, the UAW has lost nearly sixty percent of its membership, 78,000 workers since 2002.[36]

In order to avoid stateside unions, Ford shares a 279 acre stamping plant in Hermosillo, Mexico with Mazda. Ford and its suppliers are investing another $9.2 billion dollars there in addition to the amount of their initial investment.[37] In particular, the assembly of small or subcompact cars is not feasible in unionized stateside plants, which is why the Chevy Aveo is made in South Korea.[38]

Every significant piece of immigration legislation enacted by Congress since the Civil War has had the union imprimatur.[39] However, by the 1990s, organized labor could no longer convince average the American worker to become a union member. (Many equate organized labor with organized crime). By the new millennium, about half of all government employees were unionized, compared to less than ten percent in the private sector. The biggest unions represent postal workers, teachers, police officers, and garbage collectors.[40]

Labor was looking for some way to rebuild its sagging membership when those who were left out for so long started to look good — uneducated, unskilled Hispanics, so long as the new member/workers are legal.[41] In 1993, the AFL-CIO reversed its historical position on immigration. By 1999, organized labor realized that it needed Mexican recruits in order to survive.[42] Now, U.S. labor unions are actually organizing in the *maquiladoras* on the Mexican side of the border.[43]

Free-Range Trucking

One faction of organized labor that has not gone along with other unions is the Teamsters Union. NAFTA's original plan called for trucking companies from both countries to have "free range" on both sides of the border. U.S. operators have never shown any interest in penetrating into Mexico, but complain about Mexican trucks that might someday penetrate into the United States.

Implementation of the free range plan has been stalled for many years. Ralph Nader, the Teamsters, and their allies in Congress claimed that Mexicans trucks were unsafe and environmentally unsound. (Most of the pollution from the trucks comes while they are waiting in long lines to be inspected by U.S. Customs. It doesn't matter which nation the carriers hail from.)

Customs has estimated that if all trucking at the Mexican-American border could be inspected, traffic would back up all the way to Mexico City within two weeks.[44] The Nixon Administration tried to beef-up inspections during Operation Intercept in 1969. The operation only lasted a few days due to complaints from private sector truckers.[45]

Nader's watchdog publication, *Public Citizen*, claimed that the older Mexican drayage trucks (trucks that go back and forth between Mexican and American terminals on the border) were only spot-checked due to a shortage of state and federal safety inspectors. That is true, but the American trucks were only spot-checked as well. The questionable condition of the *short* haul Mexican trucks was used by the Teamsters Union to convince the Department of Transportation, Congress, and the American people of the seriousness of the safety issues on *long* haul trucks. These specious arguments also avoid discussion of the fact that organized labor drives up the cost of goods and services to consumers, wiping out some of the benefits that NAFTA was meant to offer.

During this interim period, Mexico has profited from the arrangement. Most of the terminals (and inspectors) where goods have to be offloaded from American trucks and onto Mexican trucks, and vice versa were on the Mexican side of the border.

In early 2007, the Bush administration announced a sham pilot program that would give one hundred Mexican trucking companies the long promised free range access to the U.S. so long as no hazardous goods were being transported and goods were not transported between American cities (cabotage). This transparent requirement to "deadhead" home would negate Mexican profits and leave the U.S. market open exclusively to American truckers anyway.

Whether the program could have been profitable even with the deadheading restriction remained to be seen four years later as the U.S. government continued to drag its feet. Finally, claiming a violation of the original 1994 NAFTA agreement, Mexico responded by slapping stiff tariffs on American products destined for Mexico. In March, 2011, President Obama announced yet another U.S.-Mexican trucking agreement, but it will require congressional approval.

Notes

1 Victor Bulmer-Thomas, *Economic History of Latin America* (New York: Cambridge UP, 1995), 384.

2 Thomas E. Skidmore, *Modern Latin America* (New York: Oxford UP, 2001), 251, 254.

3 Carlos Fuentes, Introduction, *A New Time for Mexico* (Berkeley: California UP, 1997), xiii.

4 Skidmore, *"Modern Latin,"* 257.

5 Patrick Oster, *The Mexicans: A Personal Portrait of the People* (New York: Harper and Row, 1989), 33.

6 Nathan Gardels, "Latin America: Looking North or South? Erasing the Border of Time," *New Perspectives Quarterly* 18.1 (2001): 2.

7 Noam Chomsky, "Time Bombs," *First World, Ha, Ha, Ha!* Ed. Elaine Katzenberger (San Francisco: City Light, 1995), 177, 178

8 Skidmore, *"Modern Latin,"* 252.

9 Skidmore, *"Modern Latin,"* 251.

10 Skidmore, *"Modern Latin,"* 252.

11 Skidmore, *"Modern Latin,"* 251.

12 Gardels, *"New Perspectives,"* (quoting Vicente Fox), 6.

13 Peter Andreas, "The Escalation of Immigration Control," *Border Games: Policing the U.S.-Mexico Divide* (Ithaca: Cornell UP, 2000), 104.

14 Donald L. Bartlett and James B. Steele, "Who Left the Door Open?" *Time*, 20 Sep 2004: 53.

15 Carlos Fuentes, *A New Time for Mexico* (Berkeley: California UP: 1977), 160.

16 Vicente Fox and Rob Allyn, *Revolution of Hope* (New York: Viking Penguin, 2007), 65.

17 Noam Chomsky, *Chomsky on Miseducation* (Lanham-Rowman and Littlefield, 2000), 156.

18 Skidmore, "Modern Latin," 253.

19 Gardels, "Latin America," (quoting Carlos Fuentes), 9.

20 Leslie Salinger, "Making Fantasies Real: Producing Women and Men on the *Maquila* Shop Floor." *NACLA Report on the Americas* XXXIV (2001): 13.

21 Oscar J. Martinez, "The Rise in Transborder Interaction," *United States-Mexico Borderlands: Historical and Contemporary Perspectives* (Wilmington, DE: Scholarly, 1996), 85. NAFTA is not the first example of a free trade zone between the United States and Mexico. There were earlier versions of a *Zona Libre* that began between the Mexican state of Tamaulipas and Texas in 1858. In 1885, the Mexican government sanctioned free trade between Mexico and the United States from 1885 to 1905.

22 "Border *Maquiladoras*," overview, *Frontera NorteSur*, September 2000 <http://www.nmsu.edu/~frontera/sep00/feat1.html>.

23 Carlos Fuentes, *A New Time for Mexico* (Berkeley: California UP, 1997), 161.

24 "Border *Maquiladoras*."

25 "Border *Maquiladoras*."

26 Nancy San Martin, "Death in the Desert," *Latina* (February 2000): 97, 98.

27 Jorge G. Castenada, *The Mexican Shock: Its Meaning for the U.S.* (New York: New Press, 1995), 262.

28 Sam Quinones, *True Tales from Another Mexico: The Lynch Mob, the Popsicle Kings, Chalino, and the Bronx* (Albuquerque: New Mexico UP, 2001), 144.

29 "Border *Maquiladoras*."

30 Castaneda, *Mexican Shock*, 261.

31 San Martin, "Death," 97.

32 "Border Peter Andreas, "The Escalation of Immigration Control," *Border Games: Policing the United States-Mexico Divide* (Ithaca: Cornell University Press, 2000), 79, 83.

33 "Border *Maquiladoras*."

34 "Border *Maquiladoras*."

35 Peter Brimelow, "Time to Rethink Immigration," *Immigration: Debating the Issues*, Ed. Nicholas Capaldi (Amherst: Prometheus, 1997), 48, 49.

36 Jeffrey McCracken, "Ford, in a Blow to UAW, Casts an Eye to Mexico," *Wall Street Journal*, 16 Jun 2006: A-10.

37 McCracken, "Ford," A-3.

38 McCracken, "Ford," A-10.

39 Vernon M. Briggs, Jr. *Immigration Policy and Low Wage Workers: The Influence of American Unionism*. Testimony prepared for the U.S. House of Representatives Committee on the Judiciary, Subcommittee on Immigration, Border Security and Claims 7/4/2006 <http://www.cis.org/articles/2003/briggstestimony1-3003.htm>.

40 Theodore Caplow, Louis Hicks, and Ben J. Wattenberg, *The First Measured Century: An Illustrated Guide to Trends in America 1900-2000* (Washington: American Enterprise Press, 2001), 48-49.

41 Howard Fineman and Arian Campo-Flores, "*Como Se Dice* 'Realignment'?" *Newsweek*, 6 Aug 2001: 30.

42 Briggs, *Immigration Policy*, 3.

43 William M. Adler, *Mollie's Job: A Story of Life and Work on the Global Assembly Line* (New York: Touchtone-Simon and Schuster, 2001), 312. Adler presents a disturbing picture of how organized labor is destroying American business, and how they won't stop at the border.

44 United States. U.S. Customs Service, *Enhanced Truck Inspection: Report to Congress* (Washington: GPO, 1997), 5.

45 Andreas, "Escalation of Immigration," 78.

Photo Credit: Vincent Blaine

Chapter Ten

GUEST WORKERS PROGRAMS

> *The person who picks the lettuce that goes on the buns at McDonalds doesn't deserve overtime, while the person who serves the hamburger receives overtime.*
> Daniel Rothenberg[1]

THERE HAS BEEN much talk in the United States about returning to a guest worker program similar to the *Bracero* program, which lasted from June 1942 to December 1964.[2] The *Bracero* program served the United States well for almost a quarter of a century, and other countries have guest worker programs that work. With a positive history at home and successful models to look at abroad, the United States should be able to devise a guest worker program that considers the needs of employers, employees, and the public.

Talk show hosts, columnists, and radical organizations have inflamed the emotions of Americans on the issue of illegal migration like no issue since the Vietnam War. With no thought to the consequences, many Americans demand the removal of all illegal migrants, but it would be impossible to identify and round up the ten million or more undocumented workers currently in this country. Even if this were possible, the economic effects would be seen in a matter of days.

However, Americans are surprisingly ambivalent about a guest worker program. After the bombing of Pearl Harbor in 1941, the United States entered into an agreement with Mexico that allowed for the importation of Mexican workers independent of established immigration quotas. The *braceros* were recruited primarily for agricultural work in western border states and Florida, although there was also some railroad work which ended after World War II.[3]

In the early-to-mid 1950s, due to a prosperous U.S. economy, the *braceros* were joined by many undocumented workers. Their combined legal/illegal presence allowed for the continued operation of agriculture and other key industries. The end of the program in 1964 required the removal of the *braceros*, but the undocumented workers stayed on and continued to come, taking low paying jobs in agriculture and light manufacturing.[4]

The concept of a guest worker program is especially important now. Since the demise of the family farm, the United States has become totally dependent on migrant labor for planting and harvesting its crops.

Some observers suggest that continued illegal migration would be more efficient than a government run guest worker program.[5] They argue that unregulated migration can respond quickly to labor needs while a federal guest worker program would be inefficient and leave crops rotting in the field. Certainly, this would be true of the current H-2A visa program, which is unsuitable for a large scale, year round guest worker program. From an employer's point of view, it is easy to see why.

H-2A workers are governed by a myriad of federal and state wage laws overseen by the Department of Labor (DOL). Additionally, employers are required to provide workers' compensation insurance and provide housing, transportation, and other benefits.[6] Health insurance is not required, and H-2A workers, like other non-immigrants, are not eligible for federally funded medical assistance with the exception of Medicaid in emergency situations (see Chapter Seven).[7]

Recruitment of H-2A workers is under the purview of the DOL, and requires a forty-five day lead time for filing applications. Two different divisions within the DOL are involved. The Department's Employment and Training Administration must approve the employer's petition for workers and certify that there are not a sufficient number of American citizens who are willing, qualified, and available for work. They must also certify that the employment of foreign nationals will not adversely affect the wages or working conditions of American workers doing the same type of work. The Wage and Hour Division of the Employment

Standards Administration has the responsibility for overseeing provisions of the worker's contracts. The U.S. Citizenship and Immigration Service has the final word on an employer's petition with the DOL before approving the immigration status of individual workers. Clearly, such a cumbersome process will not work on any scale.

Government estimates suggest there are 700,000 to 850,000 migrant farm workers in the United States, 650,000 in California alone. Some estimates go as high as 1.5 million migrant farm workers nationwide.[8] There are only about thirty thousand temporary agricultural laborers currently working in the H-2A visa program, a very small enrollment compared to the total U.S. agricultural workforce.[9] Most of the rest are undocumented workers.

As early as 1976, Senator James Eastland (D-Miss), and other members of Congress who represented agricultural states, called for strict employer sanctions (not increased enforcement at the border), coupled with a *bracero*-type program.[10] Then as now, the relation between stiff employer sanctions and the success of a guest worker program could not be overstated.

Additionally, the goals of a guest worker program would be for the United States to have enough legal workers for agriculture with enough left over return to a manufacturing base, resume growth, and begin to address the country's high balance of trade deficit. The goal would *not* be to find the cheapest workers willing to work under the worst conditions. No guest worker program will succeed if it is allowed to abuse workers who will never assimilate, and who will never get a share of the wealth they help to create.

The following suggestions would pertain to any guest worker program, not just those in agriculture:

- United States citizens must have top priority for all jobs, and employers would be required to certify that no U.S. citizens were available to fill a job before hiring a guest worker. This could not be a casual search, but a serious effort, requiring advertising in a multi-state area, good record keeping, and verification. U.S. citizens would be paid the posted salary. Guest workers would receive ninety-five percent of that amount.

- Instead of a cumbersome and expensive federal bureaucracy, guest worker centers could be operated in each state through that state's existing employment apparatus. Migrants already in the United States could register in their home state, and continue in their domicile and in their current employment if their employer was registered in the program, or indicated a willingness to be. This would give quasi-legal status based on employment to previously illegal workers, and make the program responsive to local needs.
- At the time of application to the program, the government of the applicant's country of origin would be required to screen the guest workers for identification and criminal records. (Mexico, in particular, would need to open up more consulates in the United States.) If results were not forthcoming within a reasonable period, the migrant would not be admitted or face removal if he was already here.
- New guest workers could enter only through designated ports of entry. From there, the employer would be responsible for providing transportation to the work site. However, no new guest workers should be admitted for an initial period after the inception of the program (except for agriculture), giving those migrants already in the United States time to adjust status by registering in the program and securing work. *Indocumentados* failing to register and find work during the grace period would be subject to removal.
- Initially, the country's greatest demand for guest workers would be in agriculture. The H-2A program and the Fair Labor Standards Act of 1938 are radically different and both will require substantial compromise if not complete reworking. For instance, the Act exempts farm workers from many protections, such as overtime pay, and allows children as young as twelve to work in the fields. In some jurisdictions, farm workers are not even allowed to take breaks. A modern guest worker program should not register workers under sixteen years of age, the elderly, or women who are pregnant.

- Farm work is dangerous, but most states provide little or no worker's compensation coverage for agricultural employees.[11] Guest workers must be covered by Workers' Compensation, and mandatory participation in a minimal health savings account or insurance program should be required so that neither the public nor the private sector would suffer financial loss due to the illness or injury of a guest worker.
- Farm wages must be brought in line with the rest of the economy. Many agricultural workers shun the minimum wage because they believe that a piece rate system is better than relying on minimum wage paid at the discretion of the employer. John Sweeney, president of the AFL-CIO, has said that he wants guest workers to be "protected" by organized labor.[12] America's food supply cannot be jeopardized by non-citizens holding union cards.
- The use of labor brokers (*contradistas*) would be forbidden. Labor brokers, usually foreign nationals, are paid a lump sum by the employer, leaving them free to cheat their crews while absolving the employer of legal responsibility.[13] All transactions would be between the two governments, the employer, and the employee.
- Guest workers would only be allowed to work for a specified length of time, perhaps five or six years, with no more than one extension of two or three years possible. This relatively short term of employment would guarantee that the guest worker's payroll deductions for Social Security would go to American retirees instead of the guest worker. In effect, it would be an employment tax that would help the United States to justify the program with its own citizens.
- If large numbers of guest workers are working for one employer, transportation could be made available to discourage private purchase of automobiles. Properly registered guest workers who already own an automobile would be allowed to keep it. Other guest workers would be allowed to purchase automobiles, but any guest worker found without a driver's license, proper registration, or insurance on his vehicle would immediately be removed from

the program, have the automobile confiscated, and be removed from the country.
- Employers should be encouraged to provide basic housing and nutritious meals for their employees, for which they could deduct a reasonable amount from the worker's pay, or the workers could live and eat offsite at their own expense, with no deductions. This concept has worked well where it has been tried in the Midwest. Migrants wanting to rent offsite would have to provide proof of their registration in the program. Empowering landlords will serve to make the border "thicker," that is, extend it into the interior of the country. The effects of these stipulations would be to drive the existing *indocumentados* into registered guest worker programs or out of the country.
- Guest workers would be under contract with their employer, but there must be some provision for changing jobs within the guest worker system, giving the workers protection from mistreatment, unusually low wages, poor working conditions, or the opportunity to learn new skills. Guest workers should be able to change jobs for more lucrative work in the program during their contract period, but not for a position outside the guest worker program. Harsh employer sanctions should ensure this.
- Guest workers would not be allowed to bring their families with them. The focus of a guest worker program, and American immigration policy in general, should be jobs, not family reunification. Pregnancy of a wife already in the United States during the term of the guest worker's contract would result in removal of both adults.
- Various plans have called for migrants to learn English without showing the necessity for it. Because the guest workers would be working in the United States for a relatively brief period of time, they would not need to learn English. They would not even need to be literate. Most businesses in guest worker programs will need unskilled and semi-skilled employees, but not a bilingual workforce. The opportunity for learning English should be available and encouraged for all guest workers who desire to learn it, and a

demonstrated proficiency in English would be important for those pursuing military service or citizenship later on.
- Guest workers would be exempt from the draft, although they could volunteer for one of the services if they met the qualifications. The United States has a long history of non-citizens in the military (see Appendix H).
- Employers know that the "Texas Proviso" of the 1952 McCarran-Walter Act makes it illegal to harbor, transport, or conceal illegal migrants. Hiring the undocumented was not made illegal until the Immigration Reform and Control Act (IRCA) of 1986. However, employers also know that they can only be prosecuted for *reckless* disregard of the immigration statutes, such as *knowingly* hiring employees without proper papers, which is difficult to prove.[14] ICE should police the border, but the IRS should be in charge of policing the workplace, using clandestine audits instead of clumsy raids. Employers fear the IRS; they do not fear ICE.
- A financial incentive for the guest worker and the local community would be that a percentage of the worker's wages would be withheld and deposited in a bank in the community where the work was performed. When the term of employment expires, the migrant would receive his money back with interest, but the local community would have use of it in the interim. This should not be confused with money withheld for Mexican Social Security from the original *braceros*, which was never repaid to them by the Mexican government. This money would go directly back to the worker.
- If America had a predictable supply of migrant labor with quasi-legal status and everyone involved was protected by rigorously enforced laws, it would end the arguments about undocumented workers taking jobs from U.S. citizens or not paying taxes. It might not end the unemployment of some native-born segments of U.S. society, but it would go a long way toward ending their excuses.
- Legal status does not predict how well a person can swing a hammer, and has no correlation to economic benefit. There is a solid core of undocumented workers who represent an asset to the American

economy. They should be treated as such. A guest worker program is a way to keep valuable workers in the work force, turn illegal workers into legal and accountable workers, insure that everyone is paying taxes, and give the country a better sense of who is here, why, where, and for how long.

- Amnesty in the traditional sense—instant forgiveness with no conditions—is not suggested here. The American public will not stand for that right now. Blanket amnesty cheats immigrants who came here legally and did things the hard way, such as paying taxes and learning English. Ultimately, blanket amnesty would encourage more illegal migration, just as Ronald Reagan's amnesty did in 1986.
- The successful completion of the guest worker contract or military service, a clean record while in the United States, and satisfactory completion of naturalization requirements would allow a migrant to petition for citizenship. Migrants who do not elect citizenship would have to return to their country of origin within a reasonable time. Completion of a migrant's term of service in the guest worker program would not allow them to stay in the U.S. indefinitely, or take employment in the private sector. Workers could either petition for Legal Permanent Resident status or return home.

It is true that the employer expenses associated with a well-managed guest worker program will increase the cost of many commodities. However, that increase will be minimal compared to the cost of an unworkable border security program. The United States has tried an enforcement-only policy for years and it has not worked. It is time to try a guest worker program again, coupled with stiff employer sanctions enforced by the IRS instead of ICE.

Notes

1 Daniel Rothenberg (quoting Greg Schell), *With These Hands: The Hidden World of Migrant Farm Workers* (New York: Harcourt Brace, 1998), 230.

2 *Bracero* derives from the Spanish word *brazo*, literally "arm," but in a broader sense, "hired hand."

3 Barbara A. Driscoll, "Views from South of the Rio Bravo: Migration to the United States as a Field of Inquiry, Part I," *Voices of Mexico* (1999): 85.

4 David M. Reimers, "Undocumented Aliens: People and Politics," *The Underside of American History*, 5th ed., Ed. Thomas R Frazier (New York: Harcourt Brace Jovanovich, 1978), 407.

5 Gordon H. Hanson, "Free Markets Need Free People," *Wall Street Journal*, 10 Apr 2007: A-19.

6 Wages and benefits required under the H-2A visa program are set forth in 20 C. F. R., Section 655. 102.

7 United States. CRS Report RL31114, *Non Citizen Eligibility for Major Federal Public Assistance Programs: Policies and Legislation*, by Ruth Ellen Wasems. Also see CRS Report RL31630, *Federal Funding for Unauthorized Aliens' Emergency Medical Expenses*, by Alison M. Siskin.

8 Ed Stoddard, "Agriculture Dependent on Migrant Workers," quoting *Reuters* 1 July 2007, 22 July 2007 <http://www.furtherleftforum-blogspot.com>.

9 United States. Congressional Record, data from the U.S. Department of State, Bureau of Consular Affairs, undated.

10 Reimers, "Undocumented Aliens," 429.

11 Rothenberg, *With These Hands*, 214.

12 Sarah Lueck, "Tug of War Breaks Out Over Immigration Bill," *Wall Street Journal*, 19/20 May 2007: A4.

13 Rothenberg, *With These Hands*, 92.

14 Peter Andreas, "Creating the Clandestine Side of the Border Economy," *Border Games: Policing the U.S. Mexico-Mexico Divide* (Ithaca: Cornell UP, 2000), 39.

Live Without Drugs

Photo Credit: Vincent Blaine

CONCLUSIONS

> *U.S. policies are shaped by the interplay of influences from different regions, sectors and groups: the Rust Belt and the Sun Belt; business and labor; growers; agricultural workers and consumers, immigrant organizations and anti-immigration lobbies; ethnic organizations; church people, criminal organizations and the police; as well as groups formed to promote human rights, champion women's causes, protect the environment and preserve public health*
> Abraham F. Lowenthal[1]

YIELDING TO THE doomsayers of the 1960s and 1970s, the United States reached zero population growth, but did so much faster than was prudent. Mexico has worked hard to get its population under control and has been reasonably successful, but still has a way to go.

The United States is faced with a looming dependent population of senior citizens and a workforce that will soon be too small for their support. If natural increase were to double or triple today, it would still be two generations before the United States would have enough workers to manage production without migrant labor. Mexico is faced with a huge young-to-middle-aged population who have few prospects for work. Carefully controlled migration and a guest worker program in the United States could be the pieces that complete the puzzle for both countries (see Chapter 10). In the category of extra-added benefit, it takes eighteen years to make a U.S. taxpayer in the conventional manner, but migrants can be turned into taxpayers in a matter of minutes.

* * *

The problems associated with migration are much like those associated with alcoholism. In this analogy, the migrant is the alcoholic, but there are other players in both scenarios. Much has been written about the role of "enablers" in alcoholism. Their behavior determines the course for the alcoholic as much as the alcoholic's own behavior does.

Citizens of a host country (enablers) rarely consider short-term social, political, or economic conditions in their own country—such as a strong economy—that may be the cause of migration from another country. It is much easier to think of migration as a problem in the migrant's country. In the end, it will be the migrant, like the alcoholic, who will get all the blame for problems associated with the situation.

The difference in this analogy is that there is rarely a human face to migration as there is for alcoholism. Migrants are only viewed in economic terms, or as undesirable elements who are to blame for many of America's problems. Blaming a marginal population for much that is wrong with this country is neither intelligent nor productive.

Migrants serve a valuable function for the United States when it needs them. Their availability is an asset, not a liability. What they represent to the gross national product as employees and what they pay in taxes as consumers greatly outweighs what few benefits they might receive. Nativists wanting to end the "Mexican Plague" should study demographic and economic realities before engaging in their ethno-politics and fanaticism.

People will continue to migrate legally and illegally as long as the United States needs workers. To reduce the pressure on the border—and the expense of maintaining it—the United States needs to devise a way for people to come here to work legally. The country also needs to realize that the need for workers in a guest worker program is more important than operating a social welfare agency vis-à-vis the government's family reunification program, the nation's single largest and most burdensome form of legal immigration.

＊

The importation of labor has always been one of America's key economic advantages. It can continue to be so today. Texas Senator Phil Gramm, previously an opponent of almost everything about migration, said, "It is delusional not to recognize that illegal aliens already hold millions of jobs in the United States with the implicit permission of governments at every level, as well as companies and communities."[2]

As free agents, migrants can go to another country where their services might be better rewarded. Europe has grown tired of migrants from Northern Africa and the Middle East.³ If migration is not handled correctly, the U.S. could find itself in a bidding war with European Union countries over migrant labor from Mexico and Central America, and the cost of that labor will go up for everyone.

* * *

The United States has gone from being an agricultural economy, to a manufacturing economy, to a service economy. Now it is trying to be a cyber economy. There was a time when a son might ask his father, "What did you make today, Dad?" The father might have answered, "I made a shovel (or a fender, or a circuit board, or what-have-you). Today, the father's answer might be, "I made a spreadsheet," or "I sent a fax."

The United States has become a nation of people who create very little, and have very little to sell at the end of the day. Investor confidence will not return until the United States starts manufacturing decent products at reasonable prices. The huge U.S. trade deficit exists because the United States buys more from other countries than it sells to them. The United States used to be the world's largest creditor nation. Now it is the world's largest debtor nation. It sells little because it produces little, and few nations want to buy U.S. products.

The United States must work toward a return to a manufacturing base, minus organized labor, which is nothing more than this country's expression of the failed promise of Marxism. The United States must work toward achieving a strong tax base, strengthening Social Security, and eliminating its of balance of trade deficit with China. They currently enjoy a seven to one ratio in their favor.

These changes can be augmented with a sensible immigration policy, one which starts with the understanding that migration is a function of supply and demand. Restricting the opportunity for legitimate workers will make illegal crossings more attractive. Border security is irresistible to politicians and talk show hosts, but it ignores an insatiable demand for inexpensive labor in the United States. Politicians posture about illegal migration enough to make the public think that they are doing something about it, but they do so just shy of driving more businesses overseas.

If the United States no longer desires the workforce it has, there are several possible solutions. Americans can ask all undocumented persons to return to their homelands, and they can start doing the work themselves. In the movie, *The Border*, one character asks, "Think this country can get by without wets? You go out on some broiling hot day and pick your own lettuce, and tomatoes, and beans, and onions."[4]

It is possible that American students could spend their summers in the fields like young people do in Cuba, but it is unlikely that American parents will want their children to do that. Unless or until automation is perfected, our crops will continue to be planted and harvested by migrants, by hand. The only question is whether our crops will be grown at home or grown somewhere else, under someone else's control.

Another possibility would be to find an all-new workforce. To paraphrase Pat Buchanan's famous question, "Who will assimilate better, a couple of million Mexicans or a couple of million Zulus?"[5]

* * *

The United States must decide on an optimum level of migration that will be beneficial for the economy, and then make conditions difficult for anyone with a different agenda.

Businesses and average citizens will have to shoulder more of the burden that the border patrol can not handle, even if their numbers were increased ten or twenty fold. For instance, restaurants and movie theaters have maximum occupancy restrictions, why can't apartment houses? "Thickening" the border—making it impossible to get a job or obtain food or shelter without proper identification—would be infinitely more efficient than increased spending on border security.

Migrants come here to work, and the workplace is where they are found. It is difficult to understand why only two percent of the immigration budget is dedicated to workplace enforcement, and why the government delights in arresting harmless workers while letting their bosses go free. With a guest worker program that is accountable, the government can finally put the full force of the law behind employer sanctions. Putting the IRS in charge of workplace issues instead of the border patrol, will dramatically improve employer compliance.

* * *

The country's ability to manage immigration is one with a difficult but successful history. The United States will ignore that history if it lets the naysayers have their way. The U.S. can continue using a poorly conceived and unworkable enforcement approach to keep a much needed labor force out of the country. We spent trillions of dollars to build a Berlin-style wall between the United States and Mexico (Mikhail Gorbachev might have some thoughts on that), only to completely abandon the project in 2011.

With members of the House of Representatives standing for reelection every two years, the United States can continue to focus on popular short-term band-aids instead of focusing on long-range goals. The United States can continue to increase its national debt and balance of trade deficit. It can continue to let organized labor destroy productivity. It can continue trying to survive economically with its citizens detailing each other's Japanese made cars. The United States can continue to pursue the fantasy of a cyber economy. Or it can exercise its enormous industrial capacity, match workers with jobs, and stop borrowing from China in order to survive.

The United States faces many problems. To a greater or lesser degree, each is related to the other. Migration is tightly woven into the total fabric of the country, historically and currently. Of everything that is before us, migration might be one of the easiest things to solve if we view it as an opportunity instead of as a problem.

Historian Shelby Foote has said that the one thing America really has a true genius for is compromise, even though Americans like to think of themselves as uncompromising.[6] We shall see if Mr. Foote is right.

Notes

1 Abraham F. Lowenthal, "The United States and Latin America at Century's Turn," *New Perspectives Quarterly* (Winter 2001): 12, 13.

2 David Bacon, "Employer Sanctions," *Z Magazine* (Jul-Aug 2001): 16, 17.

3 "EU to Increase Efforts to Curb Illegal Entry of African Migrants," World Watch, *Wall Street Journal*, 16 Jun 2006: A 8.

4 *The Border*. Dir. Tony Richardson, Prod. Edgar Bronfman Jr., An Effer Production, Universal-RKO Pictures, 1981.

5 Patrick J. Buchanan appearing on ABC's *This Week with David Brinkley*, December 1991.

6 Shelby Foote paraphrased from Ken Burns, *The Civil War*, Vol. 1, "The Cause." Prod. Ken Burns and Ric Burns, Writ. Geoffrey C. Ward and Ric Burns with Ken Burns, Narr. David McCullough, Florentine Films in association with WETA-TV, Washington, Sep. 1990.

Appendices

Appendix A

THE STATUE OF LIBERTY

THE STATUE OF Liberty was a gift from France to the United States to commemorate the centennial of the alliance between the two countries during the American Revolution. The original name of the statue was "Liberty Enlightening the World."[1] The work of French sculpture Frederic-Auguste Bartholdi (1834-1904), Liberty is made of copper sheets attached to an internal iron structure designed by Gustave Eiffel, who later built the Eiffel Tower.[2]

(There is considerable currency to the idea that Bartholdi promoted plans for a similar statue to be located at Port Said, Egypt at the mouth of the Suez Canal but the Egyptian government turned the project down as being too expensive.)

The French raised $400,000.00 for the Statue of Liberty from private donations. Americans reluctantly raised $270,000.00 for the pedestal, the cost of transportation, and construction. The Statue was first offered to Philadelphia, then Baltimore, but both cities rejected it. For promotional purposes, the right hand and torch were displayed in Philadelphia in 1876.[3] With the help of Joseph Pulitzer and his newspaper, *The New York World*, the hand and torch were moved to Madison Square Garden where supporters managed to raise enough money to finish the pedestal.

The book in Liberty's left arm is inscribed "July 4th, 1776" in Roman numerals. Liberty sits on a 12.5 square mile island, formerly a U.S. Army base called Bedloe's Island. The site was chosen by General William Tecumseh Sherman. The statue, originally meant to serve as a lighthouse, faces France. The Lighthouse Bureau, and later the War Department, administered the site. A star-shaped wall built during the War of 1812 surrounds Liberty.

The statue is illuminated from the pedestal, although the gold leaf clad torch is lit separately. Until it was closed to the public in 1916, twelve people could stand in the torch. Although rebuilt, both the torch and the spiked crown were closed for national security reasons but the crown was reopened on July 4th, 2009.

Due to lack of interest, slow fund raising, and construction problems, Liberty could not be installed on the pedestal in time for the Fourth of July celebrations of 1876. Grover Cleveland did not dedicate the Statue until October 28, 1886, ten years, three months, and twenty-four days after the centennial of the Declaration of Independence. (Two years earlier, as Governor of New York, Cleveland had voted against spending any additional money on the project.)

The Statue of Liberty was commissioned as a national monument in 1924. The entire site became a national park in 1933. Restoration by a joint French-American team celebrated Liberty's centennial in 1986. President Ronald Reagan rededicated the monument on October 28, 1986, one hundred years and $230 million dollars after the original dedication.[4] Liberty closed again for one year for major interior renovations after the 125th anniversary dedication on October 28th, 2011.

Hundreds of copies exist or have existed around the world including, for a time, one in Hanoi, Vietnam.

Emma Lazarus and "The New Colossus"

Emma Lazarus (1849-1887) wrote the poem "The New Colossus" in 1883. Folklore to the contrary, Ms. Lazarus was not an immigrant, a young girl, or an orphan. She was the fourth generation of a prominent, wealthy, New York, Jewish banking family. It is possible that Ms. Lazarus' handwritten poem was sold at an auction or purchased by a patron as part of a fundraising effort for Liberty's pedestal, however, it was not written for that purpose. Ms. Lazarus was thirty-five years old when she wrote "The New Colossus," and she died from Hodgkin's disease three years later at the age of thirty-eight. She never lived to see her words associated with the Statue.

Five lines from the poem were installed on a bronze tablet inside the base of the pedestal in 1903, sixteen years after the death of Ms. Lazarus, and seventeen years after the statue's dedication in 1886. Those lines quickly became the quintessential statement for open immigration, even though they have never been official U.S. immigration policy.

"The New Colossus"
by Emma Lazarus

Not like the brazen giant of Greek fame,
With conquering limbs astride from land to land;
Here at our sea-washed, sunset gates shall stand
A mighty woman with a torch, whose flame
Is the imprisoned lightening, and her name
Mother of Exiles. From her beacon-hand
Glows world-wide welcome; her mild eyes command
The air-bridged harbor that twin cities frame.
"Keep ancient lands, your storied pomp!"
Cries she with silent lips.
Give me your tired, your poor,
Your huddled masses yearning to breathe free,
The wretched refuse of your teeming shore.
Send these, the homeless, tempest-tost to me,
I lift my lamp beside the golden door!"

Notes

1 An equally beautiful statue, "Lady Freedom," sits atop the Capitol dome in Washington, D. C.

2 The Statue of Liberty is 151 feet tall. Liberty's right arm is 42' long, her right hand is 16'5" long, and her right index finger is 8' long. Her head is 17'3" high by 10' across. The Statue weighs 225 tons. The copper skin weighs one hundred tons.

3 Frederic Bartholdi also made a replica of the flame held aloft by the Statue of Liberty. In Paris, it stands in a small park called the Pont de L'Alma. Running underneath the park is the Alma Tunnel, where Lady Diana Spencer and Dodi Fayed met their death. Many young people are under the impression that the flame is a memorial to Lady Diana.

4 During this restoration, damaged copper from the Statue was melted down to make two fifteen inch replicas which were taken on board the April 1985 flight of the space shuttle Discovery. Upon the shuttles return from space, one replica was melted to produce a Centennial seal, sold by the U.S. Postal Service, and the other was put on permanent display in the base of the Statue.

Appendix B

THE MEXICAN-AMERICAN BOUNDARY SURVEY

THE TREATY OF Guadalupe Hidalgo, which ended the Mexican-American war, was signed on February 2, 1848.[1] The boundaries specified in the treaty replaced the line between the United States and Mexico that had originally been defined by treaties between the United States and Spain. Mexico gave up all claims to Texas, which had declared independence in 1836, and ceded New Mexico and California to the United States.

Many people in the United States opposed the treaty. Sam Houston and Jefferson Davis believed that the American victory entitled the United States to more land than the treaty specified. Daniel Webster and the Whig Party opposed the treaty because they thought it would annex too much territory, all of it in the south, which would change the balance between slave and free states.[2]

Non-acceptance of the treaty by Mexico would have meant either continued war or military occupation of Mexico by the United States. The wife of Nicholas Trist, the chief negotiator for the United States, recorded her husband's thoughts.

> [I wanted] to make the treaty as little exacting as possible for Mexico. In this I was governed by two considerations: one was the inequity of the war, as an abuse of power on our part; the other was that the more disadvantageous the treaty was made for Mexico, the stronger would be the ground of opposition to it in the Mexican Congress.[3]

The Mexican House of Deputies voted to accept the treaty by a vote of fifty-one to thirty-five. The Mexican Senate ratified the treaty by a vote of thirty-three to four.[4]

However, the treaty did not exactly answer the question of the boundary between the United States and Mexico as specified in Article V. This was because the American and Mexican diplomats were using different maps, and neither map was accurate. Both nations agreed to appoint a boundary commission which would "proceed to run and mark the said boundary in its whole course," and whose commissioners and surveyors would be the final arbitrators of the boundary between the two nations.[5] The two teams were to meet on May 1, 1849 in San Diego.

President Polk named John B. Weller to head the U.S. commission, and Andrew Gray as its surveyor. He named Brevet Major William H. Emory to the dual posts of chief astronomer and commander of the military escort.[6] Most of the original boundary commission's thirty-nine civilians, plus a mixed infantry/cavalry component of 105 soldiers assembled in Panama in May 1849 for the trip to San Diego, California.

Both teams were late, and the work did not begin until August 1, 1849. A controversy immediately arose over the initial point for the Pacific boundary. The two sides could not agree on the length of "one marine league," or *legua legal*, as specified in the treaty, and whether or not the measurement should be taken at high tide or low tide.[7] The measurement was finally taken at high tide, which favored the United States.[8]

The men on the American Commission had not been paid since prior to leaving for Panama, and many deserted during the gold rush. Emory made sure that these men received honorable discharges, saying that the government had deserted them, not the other way around.[9] Despite this and many other hardships, the portion of the survey from the Pacific Ocean eastward to the Gila River was completed by the summer of 1850, and the two commissions agreed to reconvene in El Paso in November 1850.

A new U.S. Commissioner, John Russell Bartlett, was named but he only undertook one official act with the Mexican Commissioner, known as the Bartlett-Conde compromise, before disappearing for over a year with

$200,000.00 meant for the commission. Working under a temporary commissioner, Emory and his detachment worked with the Mexicans to survey the entire length of the Rio Grande (*Rio Bravo*). Both countries agreed to run the boundary down the middle of the channel as they found it, and the line would remain fixed after that, regardless of what the river did.[10] In late 1852, with the Rio Grande portion of the survey complete, Emory received $50,000.00 from Washington that allowed him to pay his men and settle other debts. He returned to the capital, and the work shut down for another a year.[11]

By this time, the Bartlett-Conde Compromise had alarmed those who presumed that the border would allow for a southern route for a transcontinental railroad. Bartlett's error centered on the difference between "Paso," and "El Paso," and in 1853, the United States paid Mexico hundreds of thousands of dollars for an additional strip of land where the grade was suitable for railroad construction. This became known as the Gadsden Purchase, and runs through what is now New Mexico and Arizona.[12]

In 1854, Emory was named boundary commissioner, as well as astronomer and chief surveyor. His job was to link the new purchase to the completed parts of the survey. There were fifty-four sections, beginning at San Diego, and each commissioner signed the other's maps.[13] The fieldwork was finished in 1854. Emory worked for two more years on his "Report on the United States and Mexican Boundary Survey." The Thirty-fourth Congress ordered ten thousand copies to be printed.

Notes

1 Paula Rebert, *La Gran Linea: Mapping the United States-Mexican Boundary 1849-1857* (Austin: Texas UP, 2001), 1.

2 Oscar J. Martinez, ed. *U.S.-Mexican Borderlands: Historical and Contemporary Perspectives* (Wilmington, DE: Scholarly, 1997), 4, 5.

3 Michael C. Meyer and William H. Beezley, *The Oxford History of Mexico* (New York: Oxford UP, 2000), 368, 369.

4 Meyer, *Oxford History*, 8.

5 Martinez, *U.S.-Mexican*, 20, 37.

6 A brevetted rank is one of a temporary nature, associated with a particular duty or period of time.

7 Rebert, *La Gran Linea*, 31.

8 William H. Goetzman, *Army Explorations of the American West* (Austin: Texas State Historical Society, 1991), 162.

9 David L. Norris, James C. Milligan, and Odie B. Faulk, *William H. Emory, Soldier-Scientist* (Tucson: Arizona UP, 1998), 83, 84.

10 Rebert, *La Gran Linea*, 167, 184, 192. The river is now highly regulated through a series of low water dams.

11 Rebert, *La Gran Linea*, 46.

12 Richard Griswold del Castillo, *The Treaty of Guadalupe Hidalgo: A Legacy of Conflict* (Norman: Oklahoma UP, 1990), 183.

13 Rebert, *La Gran Linea*, 43.

Appendix C

NON-CITIZENS AND SUFFRAGE

AN INTERESTING SIDELIGHT to any discussion of American immigration is the history of immigrant suffrage. Voting is not one of the federally enumerated rights, and the Constitution neither requires nor prohibits citizenship as a condition for voting, making it "constitutionally neutral."[1] The wording of *Pope v. Williams* (1904) is illustrative. "The privilege to vote in a state is within the jurisdiction of the state itself...provided...no discrimination is made between individuals in violation of the Federal Constitution."[2] The court used the word "individuals," not "citizens." "The Constitution is also silent on the subject of membership in political sub-divisions, as on all other matters of local government."[3] Individual states are free to enfranchise whomever they please.[4] Consequently, the United States has a long, and to many, surprising, history of voting by non-citizens.

The Homestead Act of 1862 made 160 acres of land available to citizens and non-citizens alike.[5] Scarce labor made declarant immigrant voting common in new, large, or thinly-populated agricultural states. (A declarant immigrant was one who was not yet a U.S. citizen, but who evidenced an intent to become one).[6] In addition to the importance to the state's work force and to its economy, many states wanted to increase their representation in the U.S. House of Representatives, and made declarant voting an enticement for immigrant settlers.[7] Arkansas was the last state to discontinue the practice in 1926.

Declarant voters influenced both of Grover Cleveland's presidential victories in 1884 and 1892.[8] In 1896, William McKinley printed 120,000 flyers in various languages to assure his victory over William Jennings Bryan. The twelve states with the highest immigrant populations gave McKinley a margin of 202 to 1 in the Electoral College.[9]

It is sometimes argued that non-citizens are *de facto* citizens, and should have a voice in policies that affect them.[10] In New York City, non-citizens who have children in the public schools have been allowed to vote in school board elections and hold school board office since 1979. Chicago followed in 1989.[11] Four Maryland cities, Tacoma Park, Barnsville, Somerset, and Chevy Chase amended their charters in 1992 to enfranchise non-citizens to vote in municipal elections, using residency as the only test.[12] The action sparked controversy in the Maryland Legislature, but the communities successfully defended their right to home rule.[13]

In *Skater v. Rolex* (1976), the Colorado Supreme Court, in a decision that the U.S. Supreme Court refused to review, found "it is clearly constitutional to deny aliens the right to vote."[14] However, the opposite of that logic is that it is clearly constitutional to *allow* them to vote, in line with the idea that U.S. citizenship is "constitutionally neutral," and a matter for each state to decide.[15]

One of three theories will determine how non-citizen suffrage will be determined in the future. Adherents of virtual citizenship hold that people cannot be viewed as being irresponsible until they have first been assigned the responsibility of being responsible.

Others feel that a nation devalues its citizenship with this approach, and that citizenship must be a sharply defined alternative to non-citizenship, otherwise it has no value.

A laissez-faire approach to citizenship avoids the confrontational and/or tone of the other two approaches, and makes judgments on a case-by-case basis.

Notes

1 Gerald L. Neuman, *Strangers to the Constitution: Immigrants, Borders and Fundamental Law* (Princeton: Princeton UP, 1996), x.

2 Alexander Keyssar, *The Right to Vote: The Contested History of Democracy in the United States* (New York: Basic Books-Perseus, 2000), 166.

3 Neuman, *Strangers*, 142.

4 Neuman, *Strangers*, 63.

5 Daniel Tichenor, *Dividing Lines: The Politics of Immigration Control in America* (Princeton: Princeton UP, 2002), 66.

6 Keyssar, *Right to Vote*, 83.

7 Reed Ueda, *Postwar Immigrant America: A Social History* (New York: Bedford-St. Martins, 1994), 119.

8 Richard Shenkman, *Presidential Ambition* (New York: HarperCollins, 1999), 211-224.

9 Tichenor, *Dividing Lines*, 83.

10 Keyssar, *Right to Vote*, 30.

11 Neuman, *Strangers*, 70.

12 The test of residency only, as opposed to legal status, was verified with Tacoma Park City Manager Barb Matthews by phone on September 21, 2006.

13 Keyssar, *Right to Vote*, 310.

14 T. Alexander Aleinikoff, "Between Principles and Politics: U.S. Citizenship Policy," *From Migrants to Citizens: Membership in a Changing World*, Eds. T. Alexander Aleinikoff and Douglas Klusmeyer (Washington: Carnegie Endowment, 2000), 151.

15 Neuman, *Strangers*, 63.

Appendix D

"BILINGUAL EDUCATION"

THE PREMISE AND promise of "bilingual education" is to teach core subjects in a student's native language so that the student does not fall behind while learning English. Ideally, the student will move into mainstream classes within a few years. This rarely happens. Despite lofty sounding goals, the practice of bilingual education encourages maintenance of the native language at the expense of learning English, which is taught as just another subject. The result of bilingual education is English that is not good enough for a student to get a job in an English speaking country, and Spanish that is not good enough to get a job in a Spanish speaking country.[1]

Consider a similar story about English speaking students in their first week of a Spanish class. From the beginning, the instructor spoke only Spanish. It did not take long for most of the students to figure out when he wanted them to look at him (*ojos!*), repeat a word (*repitan!*) or turn a page (*pagina!*). However, one student became increasingly frustrated with each passing day. At the end of the first week she blurted out, "How do you expect us to learn Spanish if you don't teach it to us in English?"

The reverse of that question is, "How can undocumented children learn English if it is not taught to them in Spanish?" Bilingual Education is a meal ticket for teachers across the nation, but administrators of school districts receiving federal funds for these programs have difficulty seeing things the same way as the public does. Bilingual education enriches school districts, schools, and individual teachers. The benefit to students is questionable.

Bilingual education began with *Lau et al v. Nichols et al (1974)*, and has grown stronger ever since.[2] The U.S. Supreme Court unanimously held that schools must provide programs tailored to minority students or be held in violation of the Fifth and Fourteenth Amendments to the Constitution and the 1964 Civil Rights Act. Following that decision, millions of dollars began to flow from federal coffers to local school districts.[3] The biggest problem with bilingual education is the agenda behind it. Besides teaching the three Rs, common schools should serve as agents of unification and good citizenship, not ethnic identity and division.[4]

There is everything right about being bilingual, but bilingual education leads to a multi-cultural agenda, now called "diversity," which began in the 1960s and has since become the norm. Martin Luther King asked that blacks *not* be judged by the color of their skin or some other superficial difference, but in diversity programs, differences of race or ethnicity *are* the basis for judgment.

Instead of broadening a child's educational experience, bilingual education narrows it, and uses tax dollars to do so.[5]

"Diversity is all too frequently a code word for preferential treatment on the basis of race, ethnicity, or sex, or promotion of lowered standards."[6] Multiculturalism suggests that everyone is part of some small group that should splinter away from a core identity previously defined by dead white males.[7] "Multicultural" is a precursor for "multi-ethnic," characterized by nations like Czechoslovakia, Yugoslavia, Pakistan, and Iraq.

Whether for cultural or educational reasons, or both, California voters decided to repudiate bilingual education in 1998.[8] Proposition 227 removed students from bilingual instruction unless a parent signed a waiver to keep their child in the program. Standardized test scores increased for Hispanic students statewide. Arizona passed similar legislation in November 2000.[9] In Massachusetts, one study demonstrated that the longer students stayed in a bilingual education program, the worse their overall academic progress.[10]

* * *

Immersion learning places the student into an academic setting where both the material being studied and the language of instruction are foreign. Detractors of immersion programs say that immersion programs are horribly cruel to the students, but proponents of immersion claim a success rate twice as high as that for bilingual English.[11] Immersion learning is everything that bilingual education promises to be but does not deliver.

Younger students who already know some English from playmates or from American television will learn English faster. Regrettably, immersion does not work for all students, especially older ones. Older students might profit from taking English as a Second Language (ESL) as an adult learner instead of attempting a regular high school curriculum.

Notes

1 Michael Barone, *The New Americans: How Can the Melting Pot Can Work Again?* (Washington: Regnery, 2001), 172, 173.

2 Gareth Davies, "The Great Society after Johnson: The Case for Bilingual Education," *History Cooperative* 88.4, (2002), JAH <http://www.historycooperative.org>.

3 Matt A. Meier and Feliciano Ribera, *Mexican Americans/American Mexicans: From Conquistadors to Chicanos* (New York: Hill and Wang-Farrar Straus & Giroux, 1972), 246.

4 Robert H. Bork, *Slouching Toward Gomorrah* (New York: Regan Books-HarperCollins, 1996), 300.

5 William Peters, *A Class Divided Then and Now,* expanded ed. (New Haven: Yale University Press, 1987). In experiments in the 1970s, Peters demonstrated that stressing individual differences at an early age can lead to negative outcomes.

6 Adam Liptak (quoting Roger Clegg), "In Students' Eyes, Look-Alike Lawyers Don't Make the Grade," Center for Equal Opportunity, *New York Times*, 29 October 2007/14 Dec 2007 <nytimes.com/2007/10/29us/29bar>.

7 Bork, *Slouching*, 229.

8 Michael Barone (quoting Roberto Suro), "Back into the Melting Pot: The Welcome Effects of Latino Immigration," *The Weekly Standard*, 6-13 Jul 1998: 31.

9 Barone, *New Americans*, 172, 173.

10 Charles H. Rossell and Keith Baker, "Bilingual Education in Massachusetts: the Emperor has no Clothes," *Immigration: Debating the Issues*, Ed. Nicholas Capaldi (Amherst: Prometheus, 1997), 285.

11 Charles Krauthammer, "The Key to Assimilation is Language," *The Tulsa World*, June 19, 2005: G 6.

Appendix E

ENGLISH AS THE NATIONAL LANGUAGE

> *We must have but one flag. We must have but one language. That must be the language of the Declaration of Independence, of Washington's Farewell address, of Lincoln's Gettysburg speech and second inaugural.*
> Theodore Roosevelt[1]

HAVING A COMMON language has helped the United States build a national character from many diverse elements, as witnessed by the motto on U.S. currency, *E Pluribus Unum*, "from many, one." The United States has always been an English speaking country, and many people feel that it is un-patriotic not to learn English. This is summed up by the commonly heard sentiment, "If they want to live here, they ought to learn English." This complaint is typically heard from people who have never learned another language themselves.

When confronted by a large, visible, and growing Hispanic community, it is understandable that many Americans want the United States to adopt an official language. Upon examination of the facts, however, it is also understandable why many migrant or undocumented workers do not learn English, at least not as fast as legal immigrants.

The degree of literacy in a person's native tongue is a predictor of success or failure in learning a second language. If a person is not literate in his own language, the odds of learning another language are slim. English grammar is irregular and difficult to teach, and older students have a hard time learning the subtleties.

The Patriot Act and other restrictions in some states prevent community colleges and vo-tech centers from teaching ESL to students who are not enrolled in credit courses at those institutions. Absent programs by non-profit organizations, undocumented workers have few learning opportunities. Their options are generally limited to expensive for-profit schools or religious institutions which have agendas in addition to teaching English. Lack of opportunity can override good intentions, lack of classes trumps lack of interest, and Spanish language television can distract even the most dedicated learner of English.

For whatever the reason, first-generation migrants will learn little English, but English fluency is nearly ninety percent for adults in the second generation, higher yet in the third generation.[2] Few third generation members of any ethnic group will know their family's native language unless it was consistently spoken in the home or they learned it in school.

* * *

The Constitution is silent on the subject of language, and the issue of a national language did not come before Congress until 1996.[3] Generally, there is no movement to legislate for an official language unless that language is weak.[4] English is not weak in the United States.

Groups like English First and U.S. English support legislation for a constitutional amendment that will make English the official language. Opponents of this movement point out that more than ninety-five percent of all United States residents already speak English.[5] It is unlikely that any effort by a five percent minority will convince the ninety-five percent majority to switch sides.

Thirty of the fifty states have laws that mandate the use of English for official state business.[6] These laws only apply to the level of government passing the law; they do not affect higher or lower levels of government, or the commercial sector (businesses *can* legally enforce English-only rules if they can demonstrate a business necessity.[7]) These laws also do not affect private life. In any event, legislation never changes attitudes or behaviors.

Should a doctor in a state-run hospital in a state with official English legislation be required to give medical care only in English, even if his patient speaks another language? What about notification to residents about potential floods, impending storms, escaped convicts, or some other public safety issue? Should non-English speakers be provided with interpreters in court? Should government provide 9-11 services in languages other than English? What if a non-English speaking person was trying to report that his house was on fire? Might not that blaze quickly spread and endanger nearby properties? What if a non-English speaking person was trying to report that *your* house was on fire?

Thanks to the *barrio* / borderlands phenomenon, there will always be Spanish spoken in the United States, just as there will always be English spoken in Mexico and Latin America. English is the *lingua franca* of the world, to include the Internet. Instead of *demanding* English, it makes more sense to *encourage* it.

Notes

1 Robert D. King (quoting Theodore Roosevelt), "Should English Be the Law?" *Atlantic Monthly* (Apr 1997): 55.

2 Pew Hispanic Center Advisory, 29 Nov 2007, 29 Nov 2007 <http://www.pewhispanic.org>.

3 King, "Should English," 2.

4 Jonathon Pool, "The Official Language Problem," *American Political Science Review* 85.2 (1991): 495.

5 Stephanie Armour, "English-Only Workplaces Spark Lawsuits," *USA Today*, 15 July 2007: 1.

6 Scott T. Shad, "America's National Language," *Imagen* (July 2000): 17.

7 Armour, "English-Only," 1.

Appendix F

SAMPLE QUESTIONS FROM THE UNITED STATES CITIZENSHIP EXAM

1. Who was the principle author of the Declaration of Independence?
2. What is the highest law of the United States of America?
3. What was the first Constitution of the United States called?
4. In what year was the Constitution written?
5. What is the introduction to the Constitution called?
6. How many amendments are there to the Constitution?
7. Name three rights guaranteed by the Bill of Rights.
8. What is the most important right granted to U.S. citizens?
9. How many branches are there in American government?
10. How many senators are in Congress?
11. For how long are senators elected?
12. Name the senators from your state.
13. For how long are representatives elected?
14. How many Supreme Court Justices are there?
15. Who selects the Supreme Court Justices?
16. Who is the Chief Justice of the Supreme Court?
17. Name the thirteen original colonies.
18. What do the stripes on the flag mean?
19. Name one of the requirements to become President of the United States.
20. When is the president inaugurated?

ANSWERS TO THE SAMPLE CITIZENSHIP QUESTIONS

1. Thomas Jefferson
2. The Constitution
3. The Articles of Confederation
4. 1787
5. The Preamble
6. There are twenty-six or twenty-seven. Only twenty-six are active because the Eighteenth Amendment (prohibition) was repealed by the Twenty-first Amendment.
7. The best known rights are freedom of speech, press, religion, and peaceable assembly. Other rights include the right to petition for a change in government, the right to bear arms, the right to a trial by jury, and the right to legal council. Protections include the right against self incrimination, the right against being tried twice for the same crime, protection from cruel or unusual punishment, protection against unlawful search and seizure, and protection against having soldiers quartered in your home in peacetime.
8. The right to vote
9. Three
10. One hundred
11. Six years
12. Answer varies by locale
13. Two years
14. Nine
15. The president
16. John Roberts
17. Connecticut, Delaware, Georgia, Maryland, Massachusetts, New Hampshire, New Jersey, New York, North Carolina, Pennsylvania, Rhode Island, South Carolina, and Virginia.
18. They represent the thirteen original colonies.
19. The president must be native-born citizen, at least thirty-five years old by the time he/she will serve, and must have lived in the United States for at least fourteen years.
20. At noon on January 20

Appendix G

FAMOUS IMMIGRANTS TO THE UNITED STATES

(There are surely many, many more naturalized citizens who should be on this list. Omissions are unintentional and regretted.)

Miguel E. Lopez-Alegria (1958 -) astronaut – Spain
Isabel Allende (1942 -) novelist - Peru
Pamela Anderson (1967 -) actress – Canada
Mario Andretti (1940 -) racecar driver – Croatia
Paul Anka (1941 -) singer – Canada
Dezi Arnaz (1917-1986) entertainer – Cuba
Peter Arnett (1934 -) journalist – New Zealand
Isaac Asimov (1920-1992) author – Russia
Lincoln Diaz-Balart (1954 -) U.S. Representative – Cuba
Mikhail Baryshnikov (1948 -) dancer/actor – Latvia
Alexander Graham Bell (1847-1922) inventor – Scotland
Emile Berliner (1851-1929) inventor - Germany
Hans Bethe (1906-2005) Nobel Prize for physics – Germany
Victor Borge (1909-2000) comedian / pianist – Denmark
Sergey Brin (1983 -) co-founder of Google – Russia
Pierce Brosnan (1951 -) actor – Ireland
Columba Bush (1953 -) wife of Florida Governor Jeb Bush – Mexico
Jose Canseco (1964 -) baseball player - Cuba
Frank Capra (1897-1991) film director – Italy
Andrew Carnegie (1835-1919) industrialist and philanthropist – Scotland
Jim Carrey (1962 -) actor – Canada
Oleg Cassini (1913-2006) fashion designer – France
Steven Chen (1978 -) co-founder of YouTube – Taiwan
Liz Claiborne (1929 -) fashion designer – Belgium
Nadia Comaneci (1961 -) Olympic gold medalist – Romania

Celia Cruz (1924-2003) salsa singer; Ellis Island Medal of Honor winner – Cuba
Yvonne de Carlo (1922-2007) actress – Canada
Franklin Chang-Diaz (1950 -) astronaut – Costa Rica
Tommy Chong (1938 -) actor – Canada
Peter Drucker (1909-2005) business management – Austria
Sheena Easton (1959 -) singer – Scotland
Albert Einstein (1879-1955) physicist – Germany
Alfred Eisenstaedt (1898-1955) photographer – Prussia
Gloria Estefan (1957 -) singer – Cuba
Patrick Ewing (1962 -) basketball player – Jamaica
Enrico Fermi (1901-1954) physicist – Italy
Siegfried Fischbacher (1939 -) (Siegfried and Roy) – Germany
Glenn Ford (1916-2006) actor – Canada
Michael J. Fox (1961 -) actor – Canada
Daisy Fuentes (1966 -) actress/model - Cuba
John Kenneth Galbraith (1908-2006) economist – Canada
Greta Garbo (1905-1990) actress – Sweden
Andy Garcia (1956 -) actor – Cuba
Roberto Goizueta (1931-1998) president of Coca Cola, 1981-1997 – Cuba
Samuel Goldwyn (1882-1974) film producer – Poland
Cary Grant (1904-1986) actor – England
Andrew Grove (1936 -) founder of Intel – Hungary
David Ho (1952 -) AIDS researcher, *Time Magazine* "Man of the Year," 1996 – Taiwan
Bob Hope (1903-2004) comedian – England
Roy Horn (1944 -) (Siegfried and Roy) – Germany
Vladimir Horowitz (1903-1989) pianist – Russia
Peter Jennings (1938-2005) journalist – Canada
Bela Karolyi (1942 -) gymnastic coach, U.S. Olympic team – Romania
Elia Kazan (1909-2003) film director – Turkey
Clark Kent (1935 -) aka Superman – Krypton (renounced U.S. citizenship in 2011)

Sergei Krushchev (1935 -) son of Soviet Premier Nikita Krushchev – Russia
Angela Lansbury (1925 -) actress – England
John Leguizamo (1964 -) actor and comedian – Colombia
Ivan Lendl (1960 -) tennis player – Czechoslovakia
Ileana Ros-Lehtinen (1952 -) U.S. Representative - Cuba
Art Linkletter (1912 -) author and television personality – Canada
Bela Lugosi (1882-1956) actor – Romania
Yo Yo Ma (1955 -) cellist – France
Ann Margaret (1941 -) actress – Sweden
Juan Marichal (1937 -) baseball player – Dominican Republic
Rosario Marin (1958 -) U.S. Treasurer - Cuba
Mel Martinez (1946 -) U.S. Representative - Cuba
Peter Max (1937 -) artist – Germany
Mario Molina (1943 -) Nobel Prize in chemistry, 1995 – Mexico
Alanis Morissette (1974 -) singer – Canada
John Muir (1838-1914) founder of the Sierra Club – Scotland
Rupert Murdock (1931 -) publisher – Australia
Martina Navratilova (1956 -) tennis star – Czechoslovakia
Mike Nichols (1931 -) film director – Germany
Carl Norden (1980-1965) inventor of the Norden bomb sight – Holland
Carlos Noriega (1959 -) astronaut – Peru
Severo Ochoa (1905-1993) Nobel Prize for medicine, 1959 – Spain
Hakeem Olajuwon (1963 -) basketball star – Nigeria
Claes Oldenburg (1929 -) sculptor – Sweden
Pierre Omidyar (1967 -) founder of eBay – France
I. M. Pei (1917 -) architect – China
Andre Previn (1929 -) pianist and conductor – Germany
Wolfgang Puck (1949 -) chef – Austria
Albert Pujols (1980 -) baseball player – Dominican Republic
Anthony Quinn (1915-2001) actor – Mexico
Ayn Rand (1905-1982) author – Russia
Helen Reddy (1941 -) singer – Australia

Oscar de la Renta (1932 -) fashion designer – Dominican Republic
Hyman Rickover (1898-1996) admiral, U.S. Navy – Poland
Abe Rosenthal (1922-2006) executive editor, *New York Times* – Canada
Arthur Rubinstein (1887-1982) pianist – Poland
Albert Sabin (1906-1993) polio vaccine – Poland
Alberto Salazar (1958 -) marathoner - Cuba
Carlos Santana (1947 -) musician – Mexico
Monica Seles (1973 -) tennis star – Yugoslavia
Gene Simmons (1949 -) musician – Israel
Yakov Smirnoff (1951 -) comedian – Russia
Annika Sorrenstam (1970 -) golfer – Sweden
George Soros (1930 -) financier – Hungary
Sammy Sosa (1958 -) baseball player - Dominican Republic
Arnold Schwarzenegger (1947 -) actor and politician - Austria
Edward Teller (1908-2003) "Father of the H-Bomb" – Hungary
Alex Trebek (1940 -) game show host – Canada
Eddie van Halen (1955 -) musician –The Netherlands
Ruben Vives (1979 -) Pulitzer Prize winner, 2011 – Guatemala
Diane von Furstenberg (1946 -) fashion designer – Belgium
Werner von Braun (1912-1977) scientist – Germany
An Wang (1941) Wang Laboratories, philanthropist – China
Billy Wilder (1906-2002) film director – Austria
Jerry Yang (1968 -) co-founder of Yahoo – Taiwan

Appendix H

NOT ALL AMERICAN HEROES HAVE BEEN AMERICAN

EVER SINCE THE Marquis de Lafayette volunteered his services to George Washington during the American Revolution, non-citizens have served honorably in the U.S. armed forces.[1] Immigrants and first generation sons of immigrants have numbered high among Medal of Honor winners.

Non-citizens were designated for conscription during the Spanish-American War and World War I. In World War I, one out of every five draftees was foreign born, or spoke limited English. Non-citizens could conceivably be drafted again in some future conflict. There is nothing to prevent it.

Non-citizens may not serve as officers or hold a security clearance unless they become naturalized citizens. Navy Admiral Hyman Rickover is an example of a naturalized immigrant achieving high rank as an officer.

Potential enlistees must meet service-specific criteria, make a passing grade on the ASFAB, and demonstrate a proficiency in English, but U.S. citizenship is not required for enlistment. In fact, legislation from 1952 suggests that lawful entry is not necessarily required.

The casualty rolls in the Middle East reflect a growing number of Hispanic surnames. Marine L/Cpl. Jose Antonio Gutierrez, twenty-two, emigrated from Guatemala illegally at the age of fourteen. He was killed near Umm Qasr, Iraq, and is believed to be the first U.S. combat death of that war. Gutierrez became the subject of a documentary by a German filmmaker after it was revealed that he was killed by friendly fire.

Gutierrez was posthumously awarded U.S. citizenship by President George Bush. In 2002, Bush signed an executive order that makes any non-citizen who is killed in combat immediately eligible for posthumous U.S. citizenship.

An enduring image of the war in Iraq is the photo of Marine Corporal Edward Chin draping a large American flag over the head of a statue of Saddam Hussein. Chin immigrated to the United States with his family from Myanmar (Burma).

Currently, there are over forty thousand "green card warriors" serving in the U.S. armed forces. An expedited naturalization process is available for non-citizens serving in the United States armed forces who desire U.S. citizenship, and more than twenty-six thousand service members have been naturalized since September 11, 2001. A special unit of the U.S. Citizenship and Immigration Service travels the globe to conduct naturalization ceremonies for service members.

Notes

1 The U.S. government outfitted a ship to bring Lafayette back to the United States for the nation's Silver Jubilee in 1826. The General toured the thirteen original colonies and took soil from those thirteen states back to France so he could be buried in United State's soil.

Appendix I

AND THE BOY BECAME A MAN

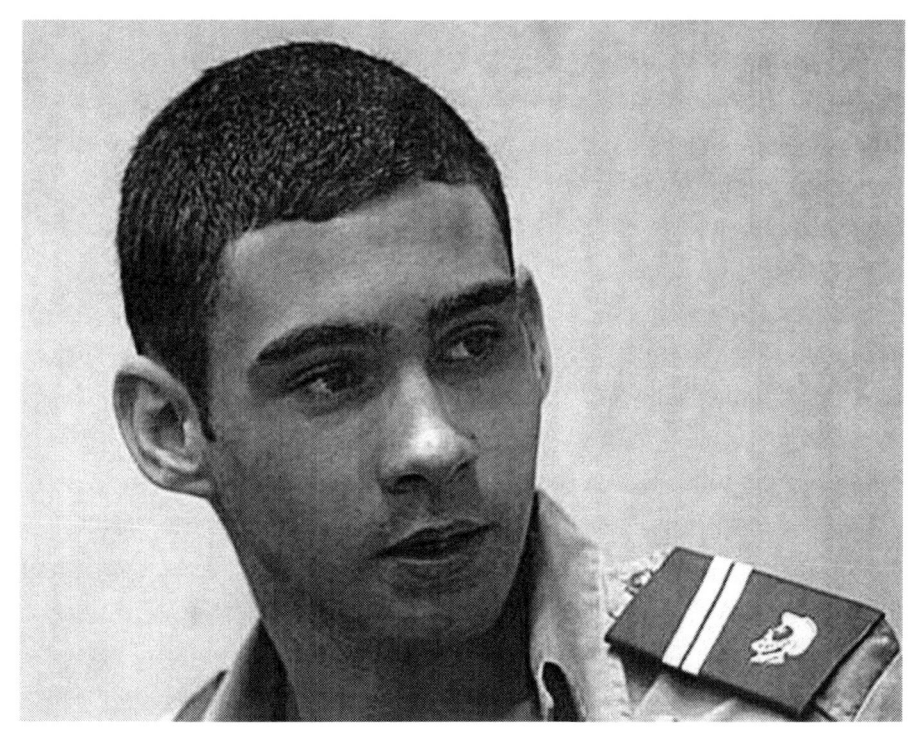

Elian Gonzalez   Photo Credit: www.cubadebate.cu

ONE OF THE most interesting recent immigration cases was that of a six-year-old Cuban boy named Elian Gonzalez, *El Milagro*, the "Cuban Miracle Boy."

Since 1994, the United States has maintained an immigration policy known as "wet foot/dry foot." If a person fleeing Cuba can make it to American shores before being apprehended, an application for admission and political asylum will usually be approved because Cuba is a Communist country.[1]

Elian Gonzalez was a "wet foot." He did not make it all the way to our shores with dry feet. He was rescued at sea and brought the rest of the way in for humanitarian reasons. Immigration officials in Florida made a mistake in their handling of the case; after a brief stay in a hospital, Elian was released to the custody of relatives in Miami. He should have been kept in a detention facility and allowed visitors, but not allowed to leave.

What followed was a gripping and entertaining soap opera where most of the players knew their parts except for Elian's stateside relatives and Miami's large Cuban-American population. There was never any doubt that Elian would be returned to Cuba. The United States is party to an international treaty that spells out exactly how children in international disputes are to be handled.[2]

At any given time, the United States has three to four thousand U.S. citizen children in other parts of the world in situations similar to Elian's. Had the United States left Elian in the custody of his stateside relatives (with felony convictions and mental health problems) instead of allowing him to return to his father, other countries would have had no moral obligation to honor their treaty with the United States. Ultimately, no American politician would have wanted to be on record favoring the sacrifice of thousands of American children for the sake one Cuban child.[3]

The Clinton Administration allowed time for Republican congressmen in Florida and elsewhere (such as Lugar in Indiana) to posture before their constituencies. Since the Cubans in Miami did not understand that the situation was just a dance of political courtesy, Elian's stay in the United States was much longer than anyone envisioned. The irony is that the United States has normalized relations with Vietnam, with whom it had a war that claimed the lives of fifty-eight thousand American servicemen, but it has not normalized relations with Cuba, with whom it has not had a war or suffered the deaths of American citizens.

The big winner was Fidel Castro. If Elian had not been returned to Cuba, Castro could have ranted about the evil United States and its treaty violations. With the return of Elian, Castro was also able to proclaim victory.

Notes

1 Roger Daniels. *Coming to America: A History of Immigration and Ethnicity in American Life,* 2nd ed. (New York: Perennial, 2002), 348, 349.

2 The United States agreed to the Hague Abduction Convention of 1980 (short title) with the enactment of enabling legislation on July 1, 1988. The terms of the Convention require, barring unusual circumstances, that a subject child to be returned to his country of habitual residence. See International Child Abduction Remedies Act, 42 United States C. $~11601-11610 (1989) ("ICARA").

3 In the removal of Elian from the home of his Miami relatives, the press inaccurately referred to his rescuers as "federal agents" "U.S. Marshals," or "Green Berets," among other things. In fact, they were members of the Border Patrol's elite tactical response unit, BORTAC. After the operation, the former Immigration and Naturalization Service (INS) decorated each member of the team for their bravery.

BIBLIOGRAPHY

Immigration General

Barkan, Elliott Robert. *And Still They Come: Immigrant and American Society, 1920 to the 1990s.* Wheeling: Harlan Davidson, 1996.

Brettell, Caroline B. and James F. Hollifield, Eds. *Migration Theory.* New York: Routledge, 2000.

Capaldi, Nicholas, Ed. *Immigration: Debating the Issues.* Amherst: Prometheus,1997.

Chomsky, Aviva. *They Take Our Jobs and 20 Other Myths About Immigration.* Boston: Beacon, 2007.

Daniels, Roger. Coming to America: *A History of Immigration and Ethnicity in American Life.* 2nd ed. New York: HarperCollins, 2002.

Glazer, Nathan and Daniel Patrick Moynihan. *Beyond the Melting Pot: The Negroes, Puerto Ricans, Jews, Italians, and Irish of New York City.* Cambridge: MIT UP, 1963.

Laufer, Peter. *Wetback Nation: The Case for Opening the Mexican-American Border.* Chicago: Dee-Rowman & Littlefield, 2004.

Martinez, Oscar J., Ed. *United States Mexican Borderlands: Historical and Contemporary Perspective*s. Wilmington: Scholarly, 1997.

Mills, Nicholas, Ed. *Arguing Immigration: Are New Immigrants a Wealth of Diversity or a Crushing Burden?* New York: Touchtone, 1994.

Montejano, David. *Anglos and Mexicans in the Making of Texas, 1836-1986.* Austin: Texas UP, 1999.

Ueda, Reed. *Postwar Immigrant America.* New York: St. Martins-Holtzbrinck, 1994.

Assimilation

Garrison, Phillip. *Because I Don't Have Wings: Stories of Mexican Immigrant Life.* Tucson: Arizona UP, 2006.

Gonzales, Manuel G. *Mexicanos.* Bloomington: Indiana UP, 2000.

Jacoby, Tamar. *Reinventing the Melting Pot: The New Immigrants and What It Means to Be American.* New York: Basic-Perseus, 2004.

Martinez, Ruben. *Crossing Over: A Mexican Family on the Migrant Trail.* New York: St. Martins-Holtzbrinck, 2001.

Meier, Matt S., and Feliciano Ribera. *Mexican Americans/American Mexicans: From Conquistadores to Chicanos.* New York: Hill and Wang-Farrar Straus & Giroux, 1996.

Millman, Joel. *The Other Americans: How Immigrants Renew Our Country, Our Economy and Our Values.* New York: Viking, 1997.

O'Brien, Soledad with Rose Marie Arce. *Latino in America.* (The companion to the CNN series.) New York: Penguin, 2009.

Perez, William. *We Are Americans: Undocumented Students Pursuing the American Dream.* Sterling: Stylus, 2009.

Portes, Alejandro, and Ruben G. Rumbaut. *Legacies: The Story of the Immigrant Second Generation.* Berkeley: California UP, 2001.

Ramos, Jorge. *The Other Face of America.* Trans. Patricia J. Duncan. New York:

Riley, Jason L. *Let Them In: The Case for Open Borders.* New York: Gotham-Penguin, 2007.

Schlesinger, Arthur M, Jr. The Disuniting of America: Reflections on a Multicultural Society. New York: Norton, 1998.

Suro, Roberto. *Strangers Among Us.* New York: Vintage-Random House, 1999.

Thompson, Gabriel. *There's No Jose Here: Following the Hidden Lives of Mexican Immigrants.* New York: Nation Books, 2007.

Waldinger, Roger, Ed. *Strangers at the Gates: New Immigrants in Urban America.* Berkeley: California UP, 2001.

Border Crossing

Aaronson, Deborah, Ed. *Border Film Project: Portraits by Migrants and Minutemen on the U.S.-Mexican Border.* New York: Abrams-La Martiniere, 2007.

Annerino, John. *Dead in Their Tracks.* New York: Four Walls, 1999.

Conover, Ted. *Coyotes: A Journey through the Secret World of America's Illegal Aliens.* New York: Vintage-Random House, 1987.

Durand, Jorge, Ed. *Crossing the Border: Research from the Mexican Migration Project.* Russell Sage Foundation, 2004.

Ellingwood, Ken. *Hard Line: Life and Death on the U.S.-Mexico Border.* New York: Pantheon, 2004.

Nazario, Sonia. *Enrique's Journey. Originally a 2002 Pulitzer Prize winning series in the Los Angeles Times with photographs by Pulitzer Prize winning photographer Don Bartletti.* New York: Random House, 2007.

Immigration Law

Aleinikoff, T. Alexanderand Douglas Klusmeyer, Eds. *From Migrants to Citizens: Membership in a Changing World.* Washington: Carnegie, 2000.

Chacon, Justin Akers. *No One is Illegal: Fighting Violence and State Repression on the United States-Mexican Border.* Chicago: Haymarket Books, 2006.

Dudley, William, Ed. *Illegal Immigration: Opposing Viewpoints.* San Diego: Greenhaven, 2002.

Holbrook, Ames. The Deporter: One Agent's Struggle Against the U.S. Government's Refusal to Expel Criminal Aliens. New York: Penguin, 2007.

Legomsky, Stephen H. *Immigration and Refugee Law and Policy.* 3rd ed. New York: Foundation, 2002.

Neuman, Gerald L. *Strangers to the Constitution: Immigrants, Borders and Fundamental Law.* Princeton: Princeton UP, 1996.

Newman, Lori. *What Rights Should Illegal Immigrants Have?* Detroit: Greenhaven, 2006.

Tichenor, Daniel J. *Dividing Lines: The Politics of Immigration Control in America.* Princeton: Princeton UP, 2002.

Labor Studies

Bacon, David. *Illegal People: How Globalization Creates Migration and Criminalizes Immigrants.* Boston: Beacon Press, 2008.

Adler, William M. *Mollie's Job*. New York: Simon and Schuster, 2000.

Breslin, Jimmy. *The Short Sweet Dream of Eduardo Gutierrez*. New York: Crown-Random House, 2002.

Pena, Devon G. *The Terror of the Machine*. Austin: Texas UP Press, 1997.

Sassen, Saskia. *Guests and Aliens*. New York: New Press, 1999.

Latin American Studies

Guillermoprieta, Alma. *Looking for* History. New York: Pantheon, 2001.

Skidmore, Thomas E., and Peter H. Smith. *Modern Latin America*. New York: Oxford UP, 2001.

Mexican History

Fox, Vicente and Rob Allyn. *Revolution of Hope: The Life, Faith, and Dreams of a Mexican President*. New York: Penguin-Viking, 2007.

Meyer, Michael C. and William H. Beezley. *The Oxford History of Mexico*. New York: Oxford UP, 2000.

Oppenheimer, Andres. *Bordering on Chaos*. Boston: Little Brown, 1998.

Quinones, Sam. *True Tales from Another Mexico*. Albuquerque: New Mexico UP, 2001.

Migrant Farm Workers

Etulain, Richard W., Ed. *Cesar Chavez: A Brief Biography with Documents*. Boston: St. Martins-Holtzbrinck, 2002.

Rothenberg, Daniel. *With These Hands: The Hidden World of Migrant Farmworkers Today*. New York: Harcourt Brace, 1998.

Law Enforcement, Narcotics, Terrorism and Counter Terrorism

Andreas, Peter. *Border Games: Policing the U.S.-Mexico Divide*. Ithaca: Cornell UP, 2000.

Carpenter, Ted Galen. *Bad Neighbor Policy: Washington's Futile War on Drugs in Latin America*. New York: Palgrave-MacMillan, 2003.

Hayworth, J. D. *Whatever it Takes: Illegal Immigration, Border Security and the War on Terror*. Washington: Regnery-Eagle, 2006.

Maril, Robert Lee. *Patrolling Chaos: The United States Border Patrol in Deep South Texas*. Lubbock: Texas Tech UP, 2003.

Rotella, Sebastian. *Twilight on the Line*. New York: Norton, 1998.

Wambaugh, Joseph. *Lines and Shadows*. New York: Bantam, 1984.

Politics, Economics, and NAFTA

Borjas, George J. *Heaven's Door*. Princeton: Princeton UP, 1999.

Castaneda, Jorge G. *The Mexican Shock: Its Meaning for the United States*. New York: New Press, 1995.

Guskin, Jane and David L. Wilson. *The Politics of Immigration: Questions and Answers*. New York: Monthly Review Press, 2007.

Population and Ethnographic Studies

Peterson, Peter G. *Gray Dawn: How the Coming Age Wave will Transform America – and the World*. New York: Three Rivers, 2000.

Weeks, John R. *Population*. Belmont, WA: Wadsworth, 1999.

Reference Materials

Clarke, Duncan. *A New World: The History of Immigration into the United States*. San Diego, CA: Thunder Bay Press, 2000.

Encyclopedia of North American Immigration. New York: Facts on File, 2005.

Immigration in America Today: An Encyclopedia. Westport, CT: Greenwood Press, 2006.

Immigration in United States History 2 vols. Pasadena, CA: Salem Press, 2006.

Films

Accordion Dreams. Dir. Hector Galan, Narr. Tish Hinojosa. Galan Incorporated, 2000.

El Norte. Dir. Gregory Nava. Independent Productions/American Playhouse, CBS Fox, 2000.

Fear and Learning at Hoover Elementary. Dir. Laura Angelica Simon. Josepha Producciones/Transit Media, 1997.

Mojados: Through the Night. Dir. Tommy Davis. Vanguard Cinema, 2004.

The Border. Dir. Tony Richardson Effer Productions/ Universal-RKO Pictures, 1981.

The Short Life of Jose Antonio Gutierrez. Dir. Heidi Specogna. Atopia Distribution. Tag/Traum Filmproduktion, 2006.

Under the Same Moon (La Misma Luna). Dir. Patricia Riggen. Fox Searchlight Pictures/The Weinstein Company, 2008.

Which Way Home. Dirs. Lorenzo Hagerman and Eric Goethals. Documentress Films, 2009.

INDEX

9-11 attack, 60, 63
abortion, 107
adaptation, 75
acculturation, 75
AFL-CIO, 104, 108, 119
agriculture, agricultural economy, 117, 127
air traffic controllers, 62
assimilation, 75-86
AIDS, 53
Al Qaeda, 62
American heroes, 159-162
American Nurseryman Magazine, xi
amnesty, 1, 80, 122
anchor babies, 23
Arizona, 83, 89, 146
asylum/ asylees, 18, 163
auto insurance, 79-80

baby boom/baby boomers, 1, 33-39
Baltimore, MD, 133
Bangladesh, 95
Banco de Mexico, 97
Bank of America (BOA), 96
Barry Goldwater bombing range, AZ, 65
Bartholdi, Frederic-Auguste, 133
Bartlett, John Russell (Bartlett-Conde Compromise), 138-139
Bedloe's Island, 133
benefits, means tested/ unearned, 83
Berlin Wall, 129
Bibliography, 167-172
bilingual education, 145-148
Bill of Rights, 21-23, 153
Blaine, Vincent, xv, 5, 11, 36, 44, 58, 75, 87, 102, 114, 124
Blair, Tony, 21
blacks, 92-93
Boeing aircraft, 61
Boeing "Project 28," 65

Bohlmann, Jim, xv
Bolivia, 61
Border Industrialization Program (BIP), 105
Borderlands, xi, 76-78, 105, 115-117, 151, 121
Borjas, George J., 27
BORSTAR, 91
BORTAC, 165
Bracero program/*braceros*, 32, 105,107, 115, 117
Brazil, 61
Brimelow, Peter, 31
Brown, Jerry, 25, 103
Bryan, William Jennings, 141
Buchanan, Patrick J., 46, 62, 128
Buckley, Thomas, xv
Bush, George W., xvii, 62, 80-81, 83, 103, 110, 159
Bush, George H.W.

Calderone, Filipe, 50
California, 66-67, 83, 89, 95, 117, 137, 146
California Dream Act AB131, 25
California Highway Patrol, 52
Canada, xviii, 65, 104
Castro, Fidel, 7, 163
Catholics, 81
Central America, 6,7
Central American Free Trade Association (CAFTA), 103
member nations, 103
Chertoff, Michael, 64, 67
Chevorlet (Aveo), 108
Chiapis, 105
Chicano(a), 8
Chin, Edward, 160
China, 107, 127, 129
Chomsky, Noam, 105
Cincinnati, Ohio, 1

173

CitiCorp, 96
citizenship, 21-30, 117, 142
  exam, 153-154
  routes to, 25-28
Civil Rights Act of 1964, 146
Civil War, U.S., 108, 141
Cleveland, Grover, 134
Clinton, William Jefferson, 104, 164
CNBC, 52
coastline, U.S., 65
cocaine, 61
cold war, 60
Colombia, 61
Colorado Supreme Court, 142
Common Market of the South
  (MERCOSUR), 103
  member nations, 103
Communists, 53, 163
"commuters," 4
Conclusions, 125-130
Congressional Quarterly, 47
contraband leaving U.S., 61
contradistas, 94, 119
consulates, 118
Contreras, Raoul Lowery, 53
CooderRy, title page
coyotes, xiii, 88
crime, 45-57
Cuba, Cubans, *Cubanos*, 7, 18, 128, 163-164
Cubadebate.cu, 163
cyber economy, 127
Czechoslovakia, 146

Davis, Jefferson, 137
Dayton, Ohio, xvii
DeBrosse, Raymond, xv
declarant voting, 141
Declaration of Independence, 134, 149
de facto citizens, 142
Demjanjuk, John, 27
Democrats, 7, 80
dependent population/ dependency ration, 37-38

deportation (see removal)
desert water project, 91
Dillingham Report, 48
Discovery space shuttle, 136
Displaced Persons Act, 17
District of Columbia Superior Court, 45
doomsters, 35, 125
Dominican Republic, Dominicans, 7
Dream Act, 24-25
driving privileges/licenses, 78-80
drug trafficking, 60-62
dual intent/adjusting status, 13
Durbin, Richard, 25

911 emergency services, 150
E Pluribus Unum, 149
E-Verify (Basic Pilot), 68-69
Eastland, James, 117
economy, 87-101
Eiffel, Gustave, 133
elderly workers, 118
Electoral College, 141
El Financiero, 104
El Milagro, 163
El Salvador, 6
Emancipation Proclamation, 26
Emory, William, 139
employer sanctions, 120
enablers, alcoholism, 125-126
English
  as a Second Language, 147, 149
  as National Language, 149-152
  Common Law, 25
  English First, org., 150
  rules for business, 150
Enrique's Journey, 6
entered without inspection (EWI), 4
equal opportunity, 91
Erlich, Paul, 3-4
E.T., 3
Eurodollar, 104
Evangelicals, 81-82, 149
exiles, 6, 77
extortion ("taxation"), 107

Fair Labor Standards Act, 118
familyreunification, 13
family values, 81
famous immigrants, 155-158
farm wages, 118
Fayed, Dody136
FED-INFO, xii
Feinstein, Diane, 93
female genital mutilation, 18
Filipinos, 95
Fifth Amendment, 22
First Amendment, 75
first/secondgeneration-migrants, 4
first/second/third world
  countries, 105
Florida, 116, 163
Foote, Shelby, 129
foreign aid, 98
Ford Motor Company, 32, 108
Foreign Trade Zone (FTZ), 105-107
Fort, Huachuca, AZ, 65
Fortune 500, 106
Fourteenth Amendment, 4, 22, 25,
  83, 146
Fox, Joseph Louis, 1
Fox, Vicente, 1, 104
France, 105
Frost, Robert, *Mending Wall*, 64
Fuentes, Carlos, 61, 95, 104
Fujimora, Alberto, 7
"further-higher," 94

Gadsden Purchase, 139
Garcia, Sergio, xv
gay/homosexual, 18, 53
Germany, 105
ghettos, 77
Gila River, 138
Glazer, Nathan, 92
Gold rush, 138
Goode, Gary, xv
Gonzalez, Manuel G.,
Gonzalez, Elian, 81, 163-164
Gorbachev, Mikhail, 129
Gore, Al, 81

Graham v. Richardson, 21
Gramm, Phil, 126
Great Britain, 105
green cards, xviii, xviii, 4,13-15, 18,
  68, 160
Guadalupe Hidalgo, Treaty of, 137
Guatemala, 6, 81, 88, 159
guest workers, 3, 115-123, 125
  provisions for changing jobs, 120
Gulf of Mexico, 65
Gutierrez, Jose Antonio, 159

H-2A visas, 116-118
Hague Abduction Convention, 165
Haiti/Haitians, 18
Hanoi, Vietnam, 134
Hazelton, Pennsylvania, xvii
health care, 76
  in emergencies, 83
Hess, Cynthia, xv
Hispanic
  capital crime, 49-50
  definition of, 7-8, 46
  marketingto, 95
  criminaloffense type, 49
  homegrown terrorist threats, 63
Homestead Act, 141
Honduras, 6
Houston, Sam, 137

I-94 work authorization, 88
Illegal Immigration Reform and
  Immigrant Responsibility Act
  (IIRAIRA), 50-51
immersion learning, 147
immigration law, general, 2
immigrant visas, 13-15
India, Indians, 95
Individual Taxpayer Identification
  Number (ITIN), 96
InstitutoTechnologicoAgropecuario, xi
International Declaration of Human
  Rights, 12
Internet, 151
interpreters, 150

Iraq, 146
Ireland/ Irish potato famine, 2
Italy, 105
Ivins, Molly, 65

Jordan, Barbara, 92
jussanguineous, 26
jus soli, 25

"Katrina cars," 78
Kennedy, Ted, xvii
Koop, C. Everett, 60

labor markets, 91
labor unions
postal workers, 108
teachers, 108
police, 108
sanitation workers, 108
Lady Freedom, 136
Lafayette, Marquis de, 159
landlords, 120
Langston University, xv
Latin America, 5, 70, 151
Latino(a), 8
Lau et al v. Nichols et al, 145
Lazarus, Emma, 134
learning English, 120, 149
Legal Permanent Resident (LPR), 13-14, 24, 26, 69, 83, 122
Lincoln, Abraham, xiii
  Gettysburg Address, 149
litter, littering, 90-91
"look alike" run, 88
Los Angeles
  Police Department, 52
  Sheriff's Department, 52
Lugar, Richard, 25, 163

Maastricht Treaty, 28
Major Cities Chiefs Association, 50
manufacturing economy, 107, 116-117, 127
Mariel Boat lift, 92
Marshalltown, Iowa, xvii

Marxism, 127
Maryland
  citizen identification, 69
  home rule, 142
Massachusetts, 146
Matricular Consular, 4, 68, 95
maquiladoras, 105-107
  in Mexican border states, 106
  participating corporations, 106
McCain, John, 82
McCaran-Walter Act, "Texas Proviso," 121
McConnell, Lillian, xv
McFarland, Brian, xv
Mckinley, William, 141
McNulty, Pat, 21
Medal of Honor, 159
Mestizo(a), 7
Mexican-American Boundary Survey, 137-140
Mexican State /Federal Police, 62, 88
Mexican House of Deputies/Senate, 138
"Mexican Plague," 126
Mexican Social Security, 121
Mexico, general, 46, 65, 115, 125, 128, 129, 137, 151
Mexico City, Mexico, 1, 107
Medicaid, 82-83, 116
Medicare, 38
MERCOSUR (see Common Market of the South)
Miami, FL, 7, 76, 163
Middle East, 127, 159
migrant farm workers, xv, 117
military service and the draft, 121-122
minorities, 91
Miranda warning, 59
Montelongo, Alfredo, xv
mordida, 79
Mormons, 81
multi-cultural agenda or diversity, 146
MSNBC, 62

Nader, Ralph, 109
NAFTA (See North American Free Trade Agreement)
Napolitano, Janet, 67
narcotraficantes, 62
National academy of Sciences, 37
National Guard, 62, 66
National Public Radio (NPR), xv
National security 59-73
nativists, 92, 97, 126
natural increase, 125
naturalization, 26-28, 122, 160
Navarette, Rubin, 87
Nazario, Sonia, 6
New Mexico, 79, 137
Nevada, 79
New York, 79
New York City, 142
Nixon, Richard, 60, 109
Non-citizen suffrage, 141-144
non-immigrant visas, 15-17
North American Free Trade Association (NAFTA), 62, 103-113
Northern Africa, 127

Obama, Barrack, xix, 25, 33, 64, 81-82, 110
Other-Than-Mexicans (OTMs), 2, 6

Pacific Ocean, 13, 65
Paso /El Paso, TX, 138-139
Pakistan, 95, 146
Patriot Act, 149
payroll taxes, 94
Pearce, Russell, xix
Pearl Harbor, 115
Peru, 7
Philadelphia, PA,133
Pima County, AZ, 90
Pont de Alma, Alma Tunnel, 136
Pope v. Williams, 141
Population, 31-43
Port Said, Egypt, 133
ports of entry, 118
pregnant workers, 118

Presley, Elvis, 60
Proposition 187 (California), 47
prosperity theology, 81
Protestants, 81
pseudo crime, 52-53
public charge, 82
Public Citizen, 109
public safety, 77
Pulitzer, Joseph, 133
Pulitzer Prize, 6
push and pull theories, 5
Pyler v. Doe, 21, 23

Quotas and visas, 11-19

Reagan, Ronald, 1, 122, 134
"Real ID," 69
refugees, 17
remittances, 97-98
removal (deportation), 25, 51-54,59, 68, 82, 95, 115-116, 118, 120
Republicans, 7, 80, 163
Reyes, Silvestre, 65
Rickover, Hyman, 159
Rio Grande (*Rio Bravo*), 66, 90, 139
Roe v. Wade, 35
Rosie the Riveter, 107
Rothenberg, Daniel, 115

Salinas de Gortari, Carlos, 103-104
San Diego, CA, 62, 65, 138
SBInet, 6
Schurman-Kauflin, Deborah, 53
Seaport Worker Identification Card, 70
Second Federal Savings of Chicago, 96
service economy, 127
Shay's Rebellion, 21
Sherman, William Tecumseh, 133
Sixth Amendment, 59
Skater v. Rolex, 142
slumlords, 77
Social Security, 36-43
    Number/card, 68
South Korea, 95, 108

Spain, 137
Spencer, Diana 136
Spitzer, Elliot, 79
Star Spangled Banner, 24, 75
state employment services, 118
State of Emergency, 46, 84
Statue of Liberty (Liberty Enlightening the World), 12, 133-134
Suarez, Ray, xv
substance abuse, 107
Suro, Roberto 63
Sweeney, John 119

tariffs, 110
taxes, general, xviii. 22, 37-40, 96, 121-122, 126
teenagers, 91
television
   American, 48, 147
   Spanish language, 150
terrorism/terrorists, 17, 60, 62-64, 104
   Islamic, 70
Texas, 95, 65, 137
   area of, 35
The Border, 128
The New Colossus, 134
"thicker border," 120, 128
three strikes rule, 46
trade deficit, 117, 127, 129
Transport Worker Identification Card, 70
tribal governments, 69
Trist, Nicholas, 137
tuberculosis, 53
Tubman, Harriet, 89
Tulsa Community College, xv

undocumented children, 23-24
United Auto Workers (UAW), 108
United Brotherhood of Teamsters, 109
University of Tulsa, xv
U.S. Constitution, 2-4, 21-23, 47, 51, 59, 141, 150
U.S. English, org., 150
U.S. Government

Border Patrol, xiii,xv, 2, 4, 6, 18, 59, 62-67, 88-91, 128-129
   operations of, 89-91, 109
Bureau of Education, 75
Bureau of Immigration and Customs Enforcement (ICE), 33, 45, 59, 62, 121
   raids by, 60
Bureau of Land Management, 91
Bureau of Prisons, 45-46
Central Intelligence Agency (CIA), 59
Citizenship and Naturalization Service, 117, 160
Census Bureau/Census (U.S. Dept. of Commerce), 7, 31-32, 38,46
Congressional Research Service, 66
Department of Agriculture, 63
Department of Homeland Security (DHS), xviii, 33, 37, 51,59, 64-70
Department of Labor (DOL), 116
   Employment and Training Administration, 116
   Employment Standards Administration, 116
   Wage and Hour Division, 116
Department of Transportation (DOT), 109
Federal Bureau of Investigation (FBI), 59
Federal Reserve, 97
Fish and Game Department, 91
General Accounting Office (GAO), 53, 68
Immigration and Naturalization Service (INS), 50
Internal Revenue Service (IRS), 95-96, 121-122, 129
Lighthouse Bureau, 133
Office of Management and Budget (OMB), 46
Postal Service, 63, 136
Social Security Administration (SSA), xviii, 36-40, 68, 95-96, 119, 127
Supplemental Security Income (SSI), 82
Supreme Court, 142, 145

178

INDEX

War Department, 133
U.S. territories and protectorates, 26

Vietnam, Vietnam War, Vietnamese, 92, 115, 163
violence in America, 63-64
virtual citizens, 21

Walker, Scott, 91
Wall Street Journal, 52, 70, 79
Wal-Mart, 63
War of 1812
Washington, George
    Farewell Address, 149
Washington Post, 96
water table in northern Mexico 107
Webster, Daniel, 137
welfare, 82
    Aid to Families with Dependent Children (AFDC), 82
    Food Stamps, 82
    Head Start, 82
    Section 8 Housing Assistance, 82
    Temporary Aid to Needy Families (TANF), 82
    Women, Infants and Children (WIC), 82-83
Wells Fargo, 96
"wet foot/dry foot" policy 163-164
white flight, 77
World War I, 159
World War II, 116
worker's compensation insurance, 116, 118
workforce participation, 87
workplace enforcement, 128

xenophobia, 11, 26

Yugoslavia, 146

zero population growth (ZPG), 34, 125
Zona Norte, 75
Zulus, 128